Making Wildlife Movies

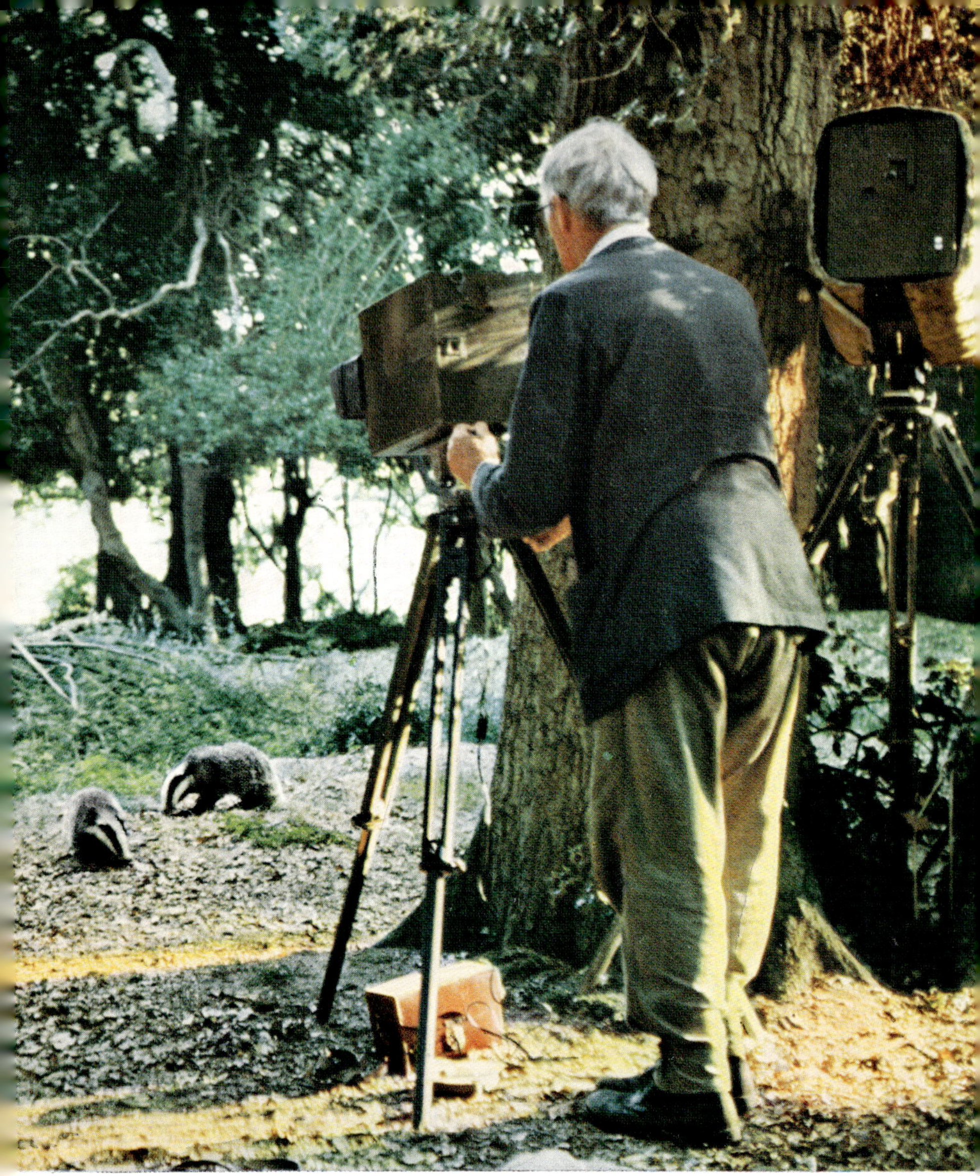

Filming wild badgers

Christopher Parsons

Making Wildlife Movies

An Introduction

DAVID & CHARLES
Newton Abbot

ISBN 0 7153 5203 2

Reprinted 1973

Printed in Great Britain by
W J Holman Limited Dawlish
for David & Charles (Holdings) Limited
South Devon House Newton Abbot Devon

Contents

List of Illustrations

PLATES

LINE DRAWINGS

1

First Principles

NOT all natural history films are taken 'in the wild', and it is perfectly possible to make a wildlife film entirely on the kitchen table. This may seem an extraordinary statement, so before going any further let us see what we really mean by 'wildlife' films. I choose to define them as films that truthfully portray, wholly or in part, animal life in its natural habitat—using the term 'animal' in its widest sense. In order to present this truthful picture the film-maker must ensure that the acts of photographing and editing do not misrepresent the animal's natural behaviour in any way. This is a tall order, but it is one that the responsible maker of wildlife films must remember all the time.

METHODS OF WILDLIFE FILMING

There are three main methods of filming wild animals. The first is to take camera gear into the natural territory of the subject; this means that an elaborate process of camouflage is often needed to prevent the subject from being aware of the cameraman's presence. The second method is to transport an animal's complete environment into a film studio, and, if necessary, condition the animal to lights; this type of controlled filming is only usually possible with small subjects. The third method, combining elements of the first two, is to photograph an animal in the wild, having first conditioned it to accept certain strange phenomena such as lights, or an observation window in its nest-hole, or a carefully arranged food supply conveniently placed near a camera hide or blind (see Glossary). It is in this third category that the most exciting break-throughs have occurred in wildlife filming during the past ten years, and as a result millions of people have been able to see kingfishers catching fish underwater, hornbills cementing themselves inside their prison-like nest-holes, and many other examples of remarkable animal behaviour.

Generally speaking, the lower the form of animal life the greater the control the cameraman may legitimately exercise over his subject. Very little insect behaviour can be filmed well in truly natural conditions since the camera must mainly be operated within a few inches of the subject, and in order to obtain large magnifications at good depth of focus it is necessary to use an illumination brighter than sunlight. However, many invertebrates can be kept in captivity for long periods and, given the right conditions of temperature and humidity as well as the correct food, continue to live their lives just as they did in the wild. By providing the correct stimuli, moreover, they can be persuaded to mate, lay eggs and feed, not perhaps on cue but certainly at times convenient to the cameraman.

OBLIGATION TO THE AUDIENCE

There are those who maintain that the audience has a right to know whenever a wildlife film has been made under some degree of control. My own view is that, unless the film is of an academic nature and made primarily for a scientific audience, the film-maker's only obligation to his audience is to ensure that his film is true to life, *within the accepted conventions of film-making*.

That last phrase is of great importance when considering

the occasional use in film-making of a captive or tame animal in place of a wild one. Purists will throw up their hands in horror at such an idea, but each case should be judged on its own merits. Take, for example, the making of a film about the attitudes of foresters to wildlife in their plantations. Suppose that there is to be in this film a sequence showing the erection of one of the special badger gates used by the British Forestry Commission in their enclosure fences. In order to prove to the audience that the gates really work, it is desirable to show a badger using one of them. Now there may be several such gates all regularly used by wild badgers, yet it may prove impossible to film them simply because no badgers in this particular area emerge until after dark. The easiest solution to the problem, and one that I would have no hesitation in using if it were really necessary, would be to find a tame badger and induce it to perform the required action in front of the camera, perhaps by the use of a suitable bait. In a film of this kind it would be both distracting and irrelevant to tell the audience how the shot had been taken. (In fact, an expert and famous cameraman, Eric Ashby, did succeed in filming a wild badger using one of these gates, and no doubt many naturalists thought it was a tame badger when they saw it on television!)

The use of a tame badger within a film solely about the behaviour of wild badgers is another matter. If it has been established at the outset that *wild* animals are featured, then you are asking your audience to accept the film as a scientific document. It would therefore be irresponsible to pose a tame badger in such a way that it appeared to be engaged in some activity of the badger community under study.

On the other hand, if a big close-up of a badger's foot is wanted, there need be no hesitation in intercutting (providing it matches visually) a close-up obtained with a tame animal. This shot would be estremely difficult to obtain in the wild, yet would make a point of some value to the film. Since it relates to anatomy rather than to behaviour, there seems no ethical reason against this device, nor any need to tell the audience about its use.

One special form of controlled filming with higher animals is the use of tame or semi-tame individuals as characters in a scripted story, rather like actors. This is often done in the motion-picture industry when a story involves human characters and wild animals. For this the 'wild' animals are sometimes reared as pets from their earliest days so that they become tame and easily handled, and they are trained for specific actions called for in the script.

Similar techniques are used in the production of some so-called 'true-life' cinema films involving only 'wild' animals. It is true that these films are usually intended to provide pure entertainment, and very entertaining most of them are; but the implication that they show natural animal behaviour is misleading.

It may prove impracticable to film certain aspects of an animal's life in the wild, and there may then be some justification for using a tame animal in a suitable habitat as a stand-in. But this must be done with caution and in the light of the total knowledge of natural behaviour in that species.

Some cinema films satisfy these conditions up to a point, but fail finally to give a realistic picture of an animal's life because the director, in order to produce action and promote box-office appeal, has crammed in as many incidents and confrontations with other species as time will allow. It may be argued that these confrontations *can* happen in nature, but it is probable that they occur only very occasionally, even when they are direct predator/prey relationships. Four or five confrontations between species that do not normally have much to do with one another give a hopelessly false impression when they are strung together in twenty minutes of film. Also, the interaction between two animals in the wild may be totally different from the interaction that occurs

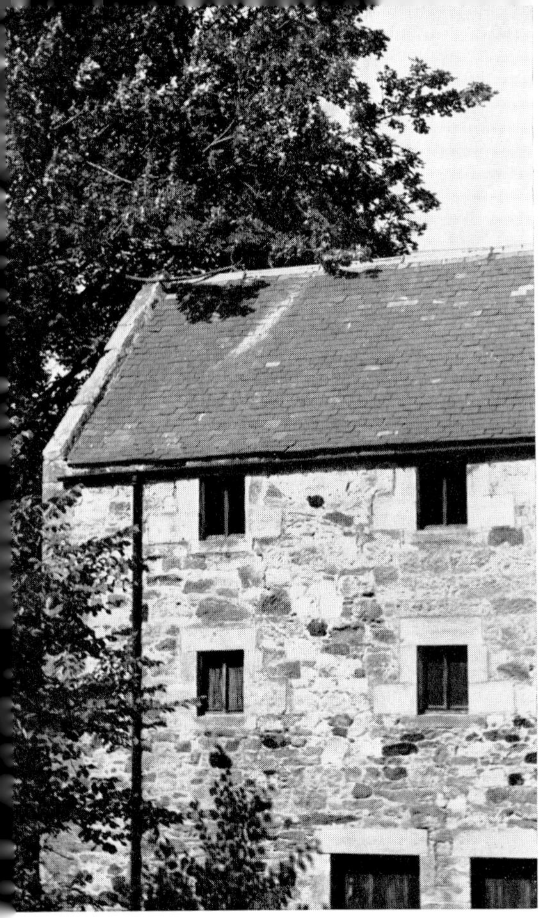

Page 17 Filming *Swallows at the Mill*: (*left*) The old mill building at Milton Mill with permanently open shutters on the top windows providing a perfect flyway for the swallows nesting on the rafters under the roof. Freedom from disturbance, and an electric supply handy for use were other convenient factors in this site; (*below*) once the birds were conditioned to the lights by starting with low-powered bulbs and working up to these two 500 watt reflector lamps, no hide was needed as the birds could not see the photographer past the glare of the lamps. Their access window is seen below.

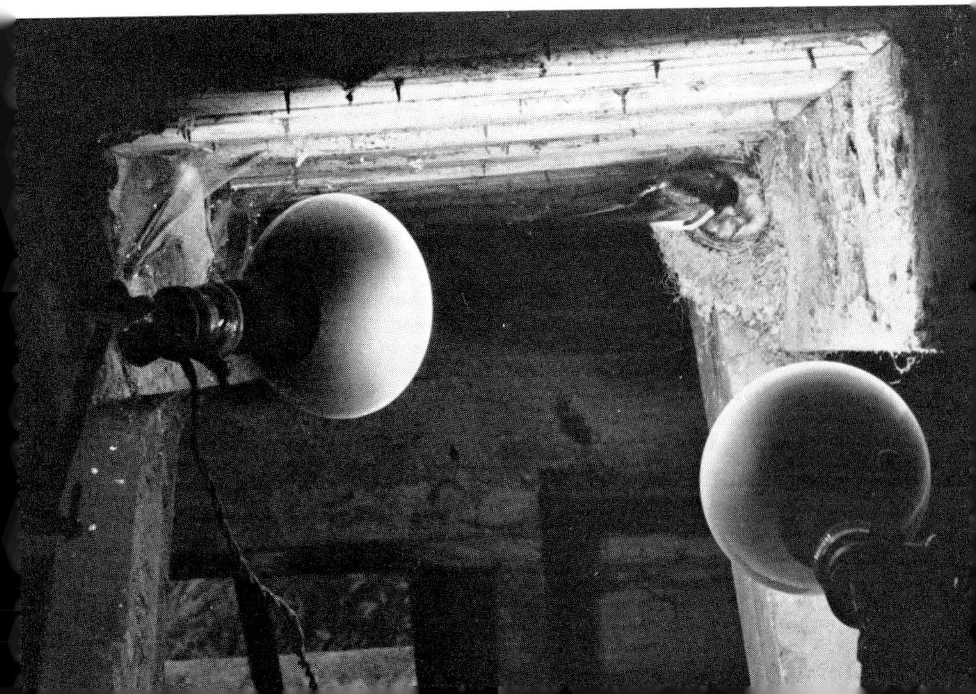

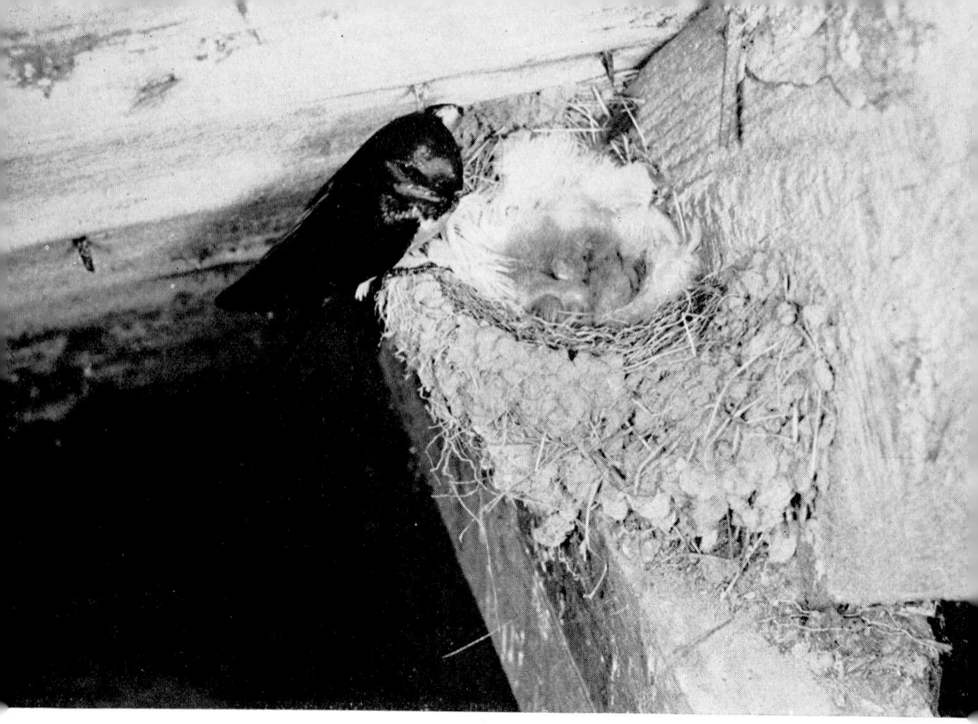

Page 18 Filming *Swallows at the Mill*: (*above*) Two nests in similar positions on the rafters were used in the film, from nest-building stage right through to full-fledged young; (*below*) brood of fully-fledged young swallows in the nest used in the film. As the nest was on the end of a roof rafter the photographer was able to sit in comfort on a chair on a few boards put across the rafters – in the darkness – and film the swallows without any real hide at all.

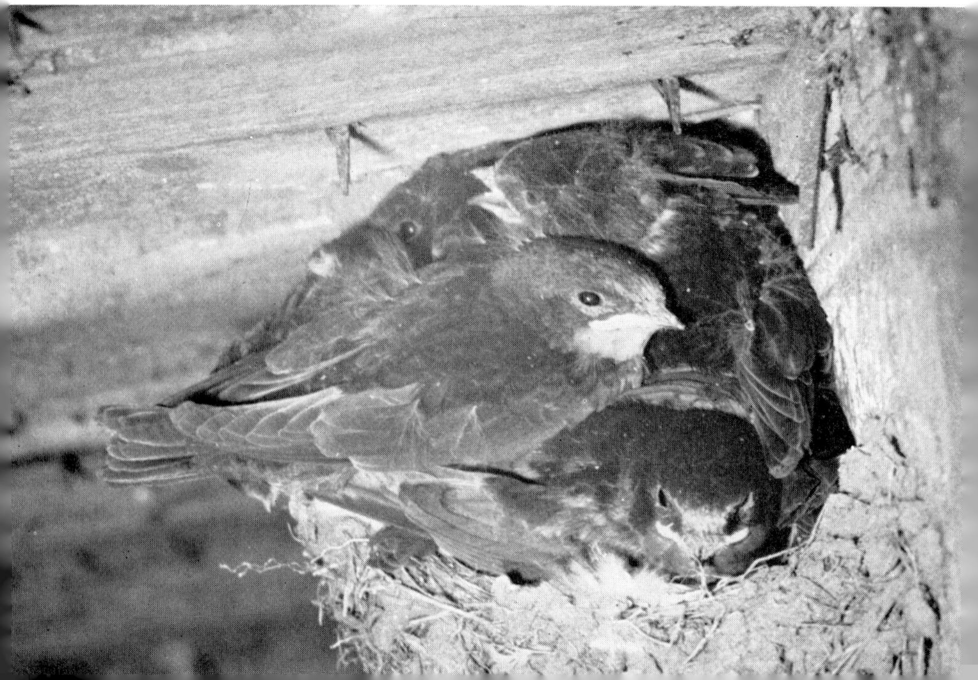

after each has been kept in captivity for six months. In the natural course of events, A on sighting B might well go out of its way to avoid a meeting, but if it has been placed a few yards from B in front of the cameras and surrounded by animal handlers its reaction is likely to be completely different. In this case, neither are the animals wild nor are we justified in claiming natural behaviour; and if the film has been advertised as a true-life document then the audience has been grossly deceived.

The film-maker's obligation to maintain truthfulness in his film, even though he is using an illusory medium, must apply to the editing as well as to the filming. A natural history film can be *absolutely* truthful only for the duration of each individual scene, but as a whole it must give a truthful *impression* in film terms.

If I join together a distant shot of a wild stag moving from left to right with a close-up of the same animal filmed the next day at approximately the same place and moving in the same direction, then strictly speaking I am deceiving my audience. In fact, every cut and join is a distortion of the truth; but if the film story as a whole is truthful then the means used in the making of the film are justified. Often only the film-maker himself can vouch for the truthfulness of his product, and this consideration must rest on his conscience.

OBLIGATION TO THE SUBJECT

The wildlife film-maker must also consider his obligation to his animal subjects. Do they, as a result of his film activities, suffer any distress or cruelty? Most people would make a conscious effort to avoid this, yet it can happen simply through ignorance. A photographer may open up a nest by removing some of the surrounding foliage in order to let in more light; in so doing he may subject the incubating bird to a distressingly high temperature in direct sunlight. The very presence of the photographer's hide may lead to the destruction of the nest by vandals, and the disturbance caused by entering or leaving the hide may give a predator the opportunity to take the eggs or the young.

We can with a good conscience witness and film natural incidents that cause suffering to animals. Cruelty can only justly be attributed to the actions of human beings, for they only are really conscious of the suffering they cause. It is futile to attribute cruelty to a cat 'teasing' a mouse, or to a snake swallowing a small mammal alive. One of the most enraged letters that I have ever received was about a sequence in a film of mine, *A Bull Called Marius*. This was a story set in the Camargue, a region of extensive marshland in the south of France, and the offending sequence showed for about three minutes the attempts of a marsh harrier to weaken and kill a straggling coot. It was a piece of opportunist shooting; we were filming something else at the time, but we became chance witnesses of a drama that went on for about an hour and a half. Our three-minute edited sequence by no means did justice to the harrier's perseverance or the coot's long struggle, but it was not short enough for my correspondent. 'How callous to film it! Could you not have stopped it?' he wrote. Of course we could have stopped it, by getting out of the hide and making a noise, but what would have been the point? We would have lost a valuable piece of documentary film and the hungry harrier would have moved on to some other prey.

If the film-maker is cleared of cruelty in such a situation, how does he fare when he deliberately introduces prey to a predator under controlled or semi-controlled conditions? Some will justify this on the grounds that it happens in nature, and in a large number of cases this is answer enough. If you wish to film a spider catching a fly, for example, or a tiger beetle catching an ant, the only sensible method is to stage-manage the incident. I also tell myself that the fly and the ant are among the lower forms of life with simple nervous systems that rule out any experience of pain as I know it. But when it comes to applying the principle that 'it happens in nature anyway' to other and higher forms of life, I find myself faltering. I have never yet, for example, introduced live prey into an enclosure containing one of the larger members of the cat family, and I am sure I never will. Somewhere between tiger beetles and tigers there is a boundary marking what is permissible from what is not. The position of that boundary varies with each film-maker. It is a purely arbitrary line, but it is necessary to observe it if a man is to go ahead with a clear conscience.

Apart from these broad principles there are no sacred rules to restrict us in making animal films. The other living creatures on this planet are important to us for many reasons, not least for our enjoyment. We gain this enjoyment in a variety of ways: a scientist may be at his happiest when he is analysing the behaviour of a particular species, while a non-scientist may love to watch the movement and shapes of animals for their own sake. When it comes to the aesthetic appeal of nature, wildlife film-makers have different ways of communicating this, just as Constable and Cézanne had different ways of painting a landscape.

Over the last two decades there have been tremendous strides in the development of wildlife film techniques. As yet, these have not been fully utilized, for advances in modes of presentation have been much slower. Since non-professionals were largely responsible for the new photographic techniques, perhaps they will also lead the way in the seventies with new and exciting methods of presenting this endlessly fascinating subject.

2

Equipment

It was fortunate that by the time natural history programmes had become popular on television, 16mm had finally been accepted as a respectable professional film gauge. At first television relied mainly on amateurs who were working on this gauge, but later, when new wildlife films were commissioned from professional sources, it was found that there were important technical advantages in working with 16mm film. Quite apart from financial considerations, 16mm cameras and lenses are much smaller and lighter than 35mm equipment, and therefore more portable and manoeuvrable. Film too is lighter and less bulky: a 400ft roll of 35mm film takes only about four minutes to pass through the camera at the normal sound film speed of 24 frames per second, but the same length of 16mm lasts for about eleven minutes.

A comparable situation exists today in respect of the 16mm and 8mm gauges. 8mm equipment is compact, lightweight, comparatively inexpensive to run, and for home use, at any rate, capable of extremely good quality results. Moreover, certain sophisticated developments in design have given the Super 8 enthusiasts distinct advantages in some wildlife film techniques.

CHOOSING A CAMERA

What is the ideal camera for nature cine work? The truth is

that it has not yet been designed in any gauge, Super 8, 16 or 35mm; even the best cameras available have certain disadvantages.

The most important features to look for in a cine camera are:

1 a reflex viewing system; that is, one in which the subject may be viewed through the taking lens whilst filming
2 ability to take a variety of lenses and associated extension tubes, as opposed to having a built-in lens that cannot be detached
3 lightness and portability, combined with a sturdy construction
4 quiet running
5 as good a choice of filming speeds as possible, within the 12–64fps range
6 battery operation for indefinite running
7 through-the-lens automatic exposure control, with manual override
8 a simple and quick loading and unloading system
9 ability to take magazines of longer rolls of film than normal (not usually possible in association with 8 above)
10 good facilities for insertion of correction filters between the lens and film gate
11 cable-release control
12 reliable film footage indicator

A wide range of 8mm cameras is now available in the comparatively new Super 8 gauge. The cost varies enormously, according to the sophistication of the model (in Britain from £18 to £480 or thereabouts). Apart from the very cheapest, all of them have features that should appeal to the wildlife film-maker, provided he does not intend to enter the professional field. There is at present little use for 8mm film material on British television – unless it happens to show something as marketable as the Loch Ness monster or the

Abominable Snowman! Even the 8mm educational loops are usually printed from 16mm originals.

Super 8 cameras in the middle price range are particularly good value. These have reflex viewfinders and zoom lenses giving everything from a wide angle to a modest telephoto shot; they are fairly quiet-running, and most have an automatic exposure control. All are light and easy to handle, and a particularly attractive feature is that they all take film cartridges that can be changed in a matter of seconds. For most bird and mammal photography, and for some insect work, they are extremely useful.

All in this price range have one major disadvantage, however, in that their zoom lens is built in and not detachable. This means that the occasional shot with an extra-long-focus lens, which can be so valuable in a wildlife film, is not possible. Neither is really close-up photography, though at least one camera focuses down to 25mm (1in), and others have supplementary close-up attachments permitting a reasonable range of insect work. One, for example, with a zoom lens with extreme focal lengths in the ratio 8:1, has a macro-attachment allowing a subject of 24 × 18mm to be focused.

Super 8 cameras with detachable lenses are rare. At the time of writing I know of only one, a highly versatile camera with an interchangeable lens mount taking C-mount lenses and also 35mm lenses with adaptors. Naturally, it is comparatively expensive. Many of the old Standard 8 cameras have interchangeable lenses, but this is of little advantage without a reflex viewing system, which few of them possess.

In 16mm there is nothing like the choice available in Super 8, but with the few cameras suited to wildlife work there are no problems with built-in lenses. For years the Bolex Reflex has been the mainstay of wildlife cameramen all over the world, and though a few top professionals are now using the Arriflex BL as their main camera, they invariably have a Bolex standing by as second camera or spare. One drawback to the Bolex is that it is quite noisy and has to be enclosed in a special sound-proof box, a 'blimp', when filming most wild mammals. Some also find its reflex viewfinder difficult to work with at small apertures. The fact that it can be battery-driven is a distinct advantage, but a much lighter power pack comes with the Beaulieu Reflex 16, which is especially useful when stalking animals. Eric Ashby now uses a Beaulieu for much of his work in the New Forest, Hampshire, and finds its viewfinder bright and clear.

LENSES

Since most Super 8 cameras have a built-in lens system, the choice of zoom lens is determined by the choice of camera, or vice-versa. This is a matter for some deliberation, since although practically all the zoom lenses have apertures up to *f*1·8 their range of focal lengths varies enormously. The shortest focal length is usually between 7·5mm and 9·5mm (giving a wide-angle shot), but the longest focal length can be anything between 28mm and 60mm. If the size of the lens is determined by purely financial considerations, a maximum focal length of 40mm is a fair compromise as this still gives reasonable scope for birds and mammals.

For much wildlife filming a zoom lens with a good working ratio is an extremely useful tool, and has some advantages over interchangeable lenses of fixed focal lengths. Though it should be used very sparingly whilst the camera is running, it provides in effect a whole range of lenses of many different focal lengths for immediate use.

In 16mm cameras the zoom lens is even more useful because it can be detached. If finances allow, a 10:1 zoom and a 300mm (12in) lens will satisfy all the needs of the bird-photographer, except in extremely long-distance work.

Because so much of his work has to be done in poor light,

the mammal-photographer must look for telephoto lenses that give good definition at the widest aperture available. He will probably find that 75mm (3in) and 150mm (6in) lenses are the most appropriate for foxes, badgers and deer, though he will always have occasional use for a 300mm lens.

For macro-photography of insects a 25mm (1in) and a 75mm (3in) lens with a set of extension rings or a bellows system will be adequate. For magnifications above life-size a wide-angle lens (focal length 16mm), reversed and fitted on an extension tube exceeding the focal length of the lens, will give good results if sufficient illumination is available.

Readers who possess a camera with only one or two lenses should not be too discouraged by this discussion of ideal camera and lens equipment. Many people only have time to study and film one aspect of natural history, perhaps just the birds in the garden or park. With such subjects, a little patience can achieve worthwhile results from comparatively cheap and simple camera equipment. But if you are going to try to film wild birds or any other form of life, whether it be a film of a few minutes or of half an hour, the one extra piece of camera equipment that is absolutely essential is a tripod.

TRIPODS

A very large proportion of all wildlife film is taken through lenses of long focal length. If your camera has a built-in zoom lens, it will inevitably be used at its longest focal length for the greater part of the total operating time, and even with the modern lightweight 8mm it is almost impossible to obtain an acceptable steady shot from a hand-held camera. The longer the lens used, the narrower is its angle of acceptance and the more important it is for camera and lens to be absolutely steady. A cameraman may *think* he can hold his camera like a rock, but when his telephoto shots are projected the results usually tell him that he has wasted his film. Only when the subject is moving fairly fast and the camera is following it, is a hand-held telephoto shot likely to be of much use.

Even when he has lenses of shorter focal length on his camera, the wildlife cameraman finds himself sitting and waiting for long periods. In these conditions the camera is always best mounted on a tripod, focused and ready for action; and in a hide, where most of the sitting and waiting will take place, it is almost impossible to work comfortably without a tripod.

It is not difficult to find a reasonably stable tripod suitable for 8mm equipment. There is however a tendency to assume that, because the camera itself is light, a light tripod will do. This is not so; the advantages of portability are more than cancelled out if the tripod is not rigid. Moreover, it has to be really robust to stand up to the wear and tear inflicted by salt and fresh water, sand, mud, rocks, dust and all the other accompaniments of wildlife filming.

There are remarkably few satisfactory tripods for long-range 16mm work, and these are expensive. Several wildlife cameramen I know have solved this problem by buying cheap, ex-government surplus, heavy-duty tripods. Usually these have been used in surveying, but the purchase of a new head turns them into really excellent tripods for the 16mm camera.

Provided it has rigid legs, the most important part of a tripod is its pan-and-tilt head. The smoothness with which this can be moved is of paramount importance to the wildlife film-maker, who frequently has to pan his camera with fast-moving animals whilst working on a long-focus lens. Heads that show any tendency to stick at beginnings and ends of panning movements should be avoided at all costs. There is no doubt that the best type of head is a fluid-filled one; the Miller light-duty fluid head has been a favourite of many British wildlife cameramen for some years now, though the larger medium-duty head should be used with heavier cameras and lenses of extra-long focal length.

For indoor work, such as filming fish or insects under artificial light, a 'spider' is a useful accessory. This provides a purchase on a tiled or concrete floor for the three points of the tripod legs. It also prevents damage to carpets.

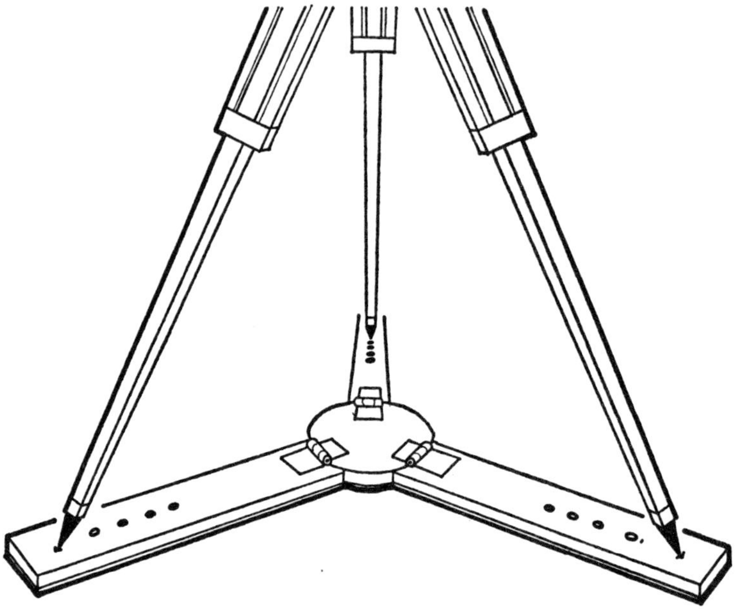

Fig 1 A tripod 'spider'

Spiders can be purchased from specialist suppliers, but they can very easily be made out of wood or light metal alloy. The term 'spider' must have been coined by someone unfamiliar with basic biology, for this one has three legs not eight; they are hinged to a circular hub as shown in Fig 1. Each leg is about eighteen inches long and has several notches at regular intervals to give a number of possible positions for the tripod. The underside of each leg can be covered with a layer of felt or rubber to provide a better grip on smooth surfaces and to prevent scratching. The hinges allow the legs to be folded up for easy storage and transportation.

BLIMPS

With many animal subjects the whirr of the camera during filming produces no problems; insects, for example, are totally unaffected by it, and the only occasion when mechanical noise causes any difficulty in the filming of birds is when the camera is very close to the nest. Usually the birds get used to the whirr after a short time, but if they continue to be upset by it, the body of the camera can be wrapped in a scarf or some other material and this ought to reduce the noise sufficiently.

When filming most wild mammals, however, even a slight click is enough to put several hundred yards between the cameraman and his subject. If any success at all is to be had, the camera must be encased in a special sound-proof box. This 'blimp', as it is called, inevitably means a heavier and more unwieldy load for the cameraman, but that is, literally, the burden that the cine photographer of wild mammals has to bear.

Although some cameras designed for sound-film work can be bought with blimps already fitted, these are invariably very expensive and nearly always very heavy. Amateurs, and indeed many professionals, are forced to make their own blimps to suit individual filming requirements and camera design.

Because the shape and position of such things as viewfinder and start button vary so much from camera to camera, it is not possible to give specifications for an ideal blimp, but the following general points are important. A camera blimp should have:

1 lightweight and compact construction
2 as many facilities as possible for controlling the camera from outside the blimp
3 a well-lined interior, padded with sound-absorbent material
4 as little contact as possible between the camera and its containing box

Fig 2 shows a blimp designed for a clockwork-driven camera. The main access door A can be opened to permit re-winding when the camera is in position. The advantage of being able to re-wind like this is limited, however, because the operation can be as noisy as, or even noisier than, filming and so the whole object of using the blimp is defeated unless it is possible to withdraw to a safe distance every time the camera runs down.

With electrically-driven cameras, especially those that take quick-loading cassettes, it is best to have the main access door on the left of the camera to permit reloading in the field.

The blimp is designed to enclose as much of the lens as possible, as well as the camera. It is no use leaving several inches of exposed lens outside the box because this will conduct and transmit camera noise. Direct contact must be avoided between the camera and the wooden box, and for this reason the inside of the lens hole B should be lined with foam rubber or a continuation of whatever lining is used for the interior. A small glass window is built into the back of the box at C to permit use of the viewfinder, but again care must be taken to prevent the camera from actually touching it. The camera itself rests on a wooden base floating on a thick rubber floor, and is kept in position by four guides, D and E at the top, and F and G at the bottom (D and F are not shown in the diagram). E is hinged to allow the camera to be placed inside the blimp.

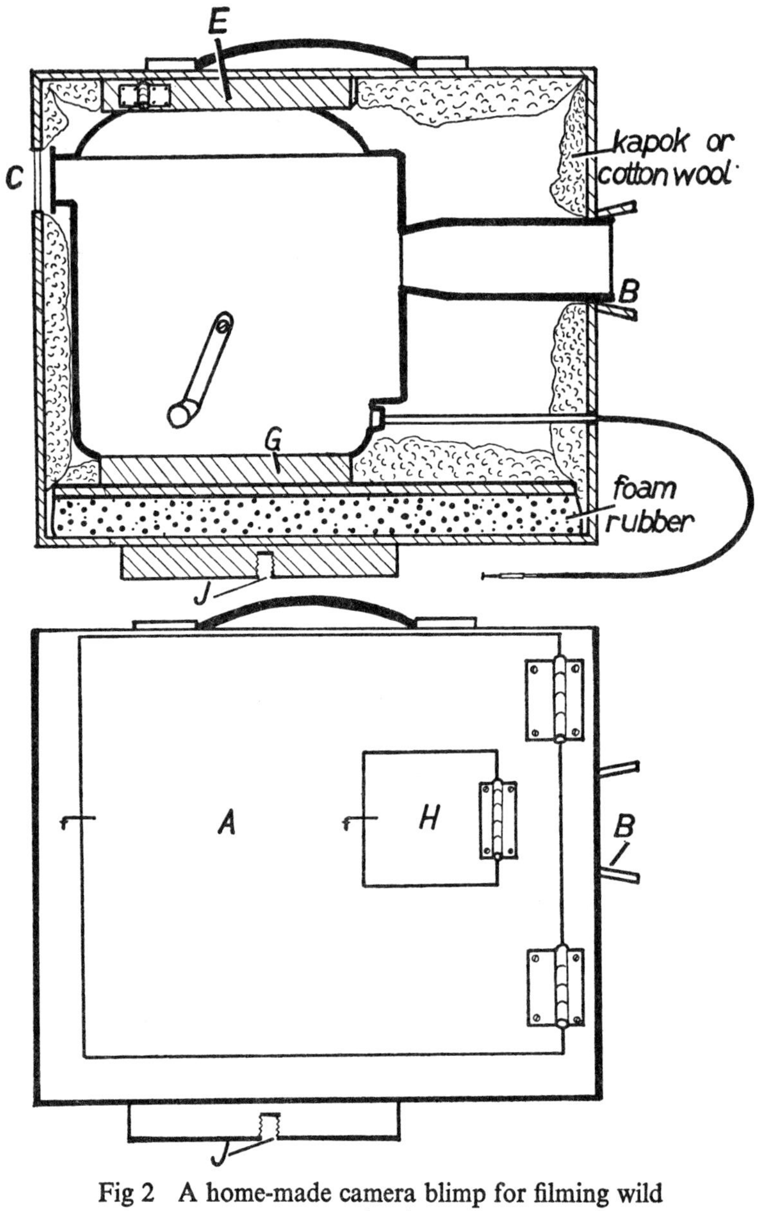

Fig 2 A home-made camera blimp for filming wild animals

A spring-loaded connector button may be fitted in line with the actual camera start button, but the best method of control is to build in a long cable release, which can be plugged into the camera after it is placed in the blimp, and which can be folded back towards the tripod pan handle.

With this type of blimp, all lens control during camera operation must be sacrificed in the interests of silence, but a second door, H, is incorporated to permit adjustment of aperture, focus and, if a zoom lens is used, focal length between takes.

All interior walls, including the doors A and H, are lined with as many thicknesses of a good sound-absorbing material as room will permit. Cotton-wool layers or kapok may be used, and these are enclosed and pinned to the walls under material thick enough to prevent bits of fluff working through and getting into the camera or filter holder.

Even with the blimp interior lined and the camera in position, there is still a considerable volume of empty space inside, and this must be filled with more sound-absorbing material. Enlist the help of someone who can use a needle and thread, and have several little bags made and stuffed like pincushions. These can then be packed around the camera when it is in position.

Finally, there is a handle to fix on top of the blimp, and a mount, J, to take the tripod screw. It is wise to leave the fitting of this until the very last stage of all, since its correct position should be found in relation to the centre of gravity of the blimp when the camera and sound insulators are all in place; otherwise the tripod head will be tilted backwards or forwards by the uneven weight distribution, and camera operating will be made more difficult.

The construction of a blimp is a job best done in the winter months when there is time for experimenting with design and materials. The general design outlined above can be vastly improved for individual camera requirements, and new materials suitable for sound insulation are coming onto the market all the time. One cameraman I know is at present experimenting with alternate layers of vinyl tile and thin foam for the inside walls of a new blimp.

HIDES

A hide, or blind, is an important part of a wildlife photographer's equipment for filming birds at the nest. We shall see later that it is by no means essential for the filming of all wildlife out of doors, but since one never knows when a hide may be needed in a hurry, it is wise to have one made before embarking on *any* project.

An all-purpose hide can be made at very little cost during the winter months before peak filming activities commence, but it is important to remember the following requirements when designing it. It should be:

1 simple in construction so that it can be erected quickly and, if necessary, without help
2 rigid, and able to stand up to heavy winds and rain
3 light and portable since it may have to be carried considerable distances
4 small enough in size to satisfy 3 above, but large enough to sit in comfortably for long periods

Cameramen usually develop individual designs to suit their own physical build and the dimensions of their cameras, but the following basic design will serve as a guide for beginners. The roof and walls of the hide should be made from two pieces of dark brown or green cloth or canvas, each about 40in × 5yd. These are laid in a cross as shown in Fig 3, the double thickness serving as the roof of the hide. The eight edges ABCDEFGH are each turned in 1in to provide extra strength for seams, and then AB, CD and EF are sewn together. G and H are sewn only for about 1ft from the corner of the roof. The unsewn flap serves to give access to the hide, and tapes should be sewn to G and H so that the hide can be closed from the inside. The bottom 11in of each side may be turned up on the outside to form four pockets; these can then be filled with stones to weight down the sides and prevent them flapping about in the wind. Rings can also be attached to the bottom corners of the sides to provide an alternative method of securing them. Finally four sets of guy ropes should be attached to the roof corners.

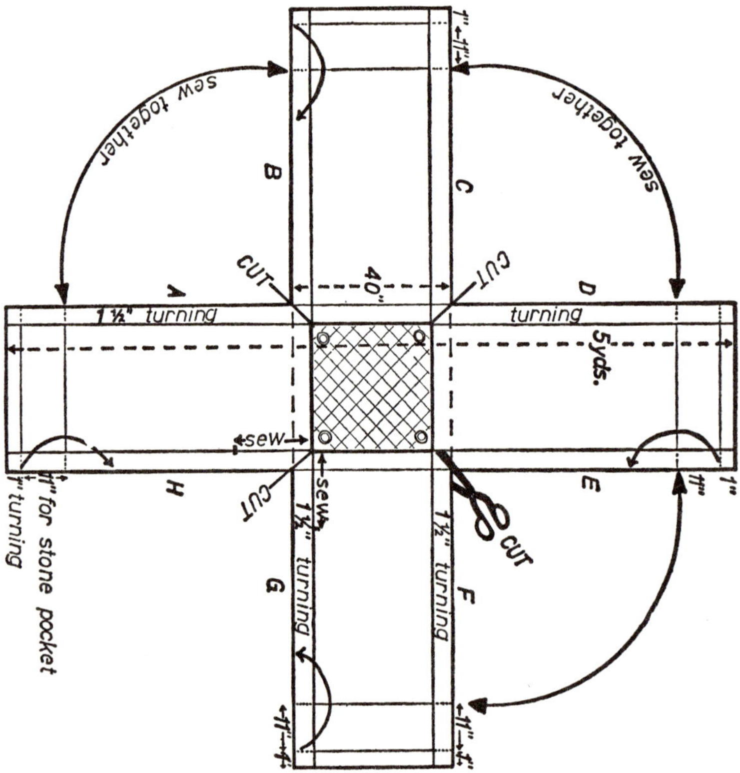

Fig 3 Pattern for a hide cover made out of two lengths of canvas

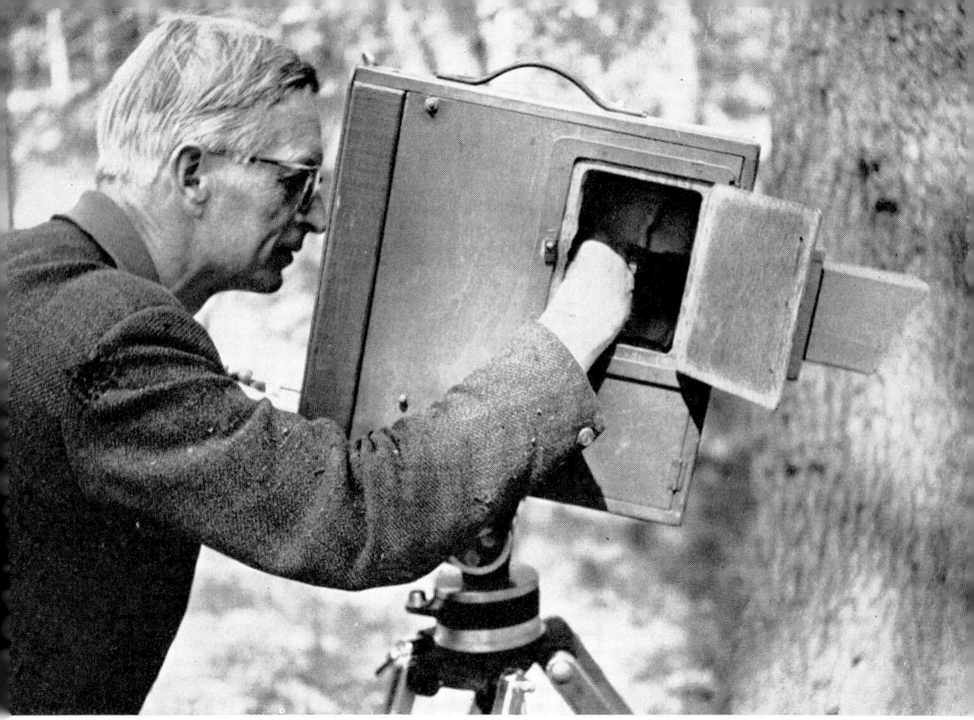

Page 35 (*above*) Eric Ashby with home-made camera blimp for filming mammals. The small open door is for making lens adjustments in the field. The main door, used for placing the camera inside, is closed; (*below*) adjusting the camera before closing the main door. Note the sound-absorbing lining. Additional cushions will be placed around the camera before the door is closed.

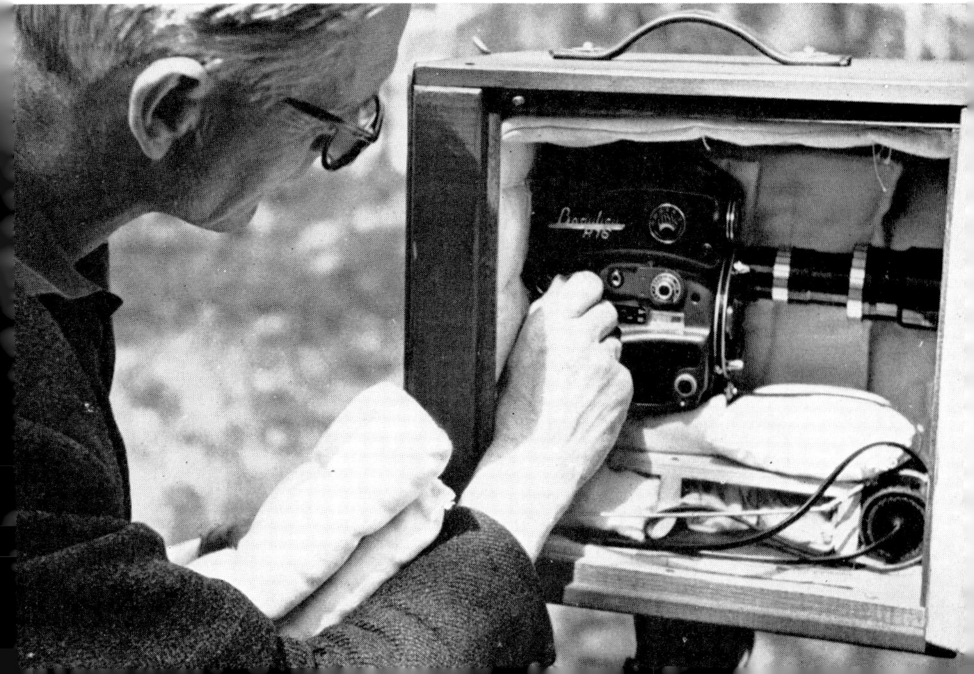

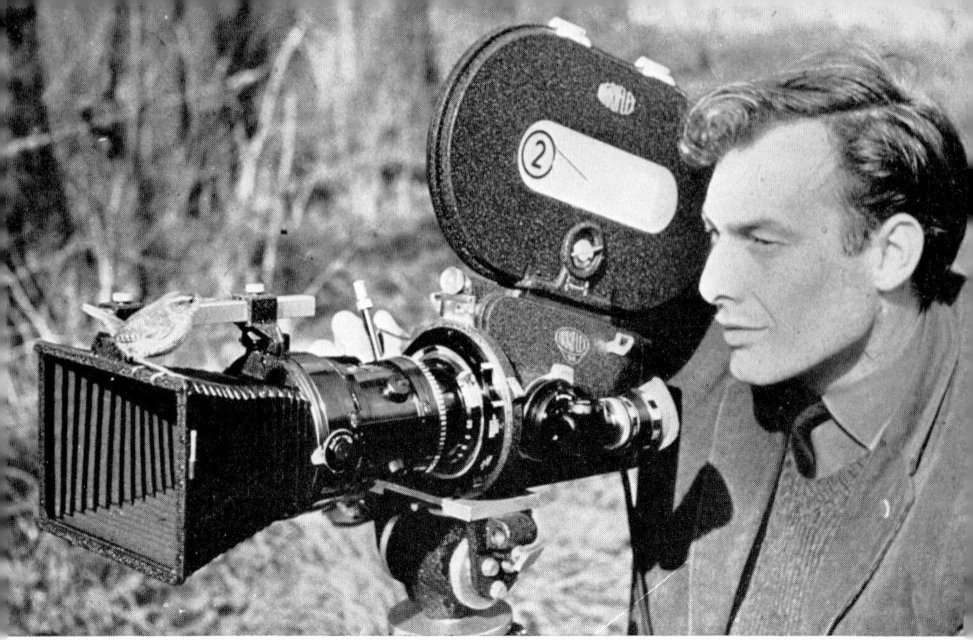

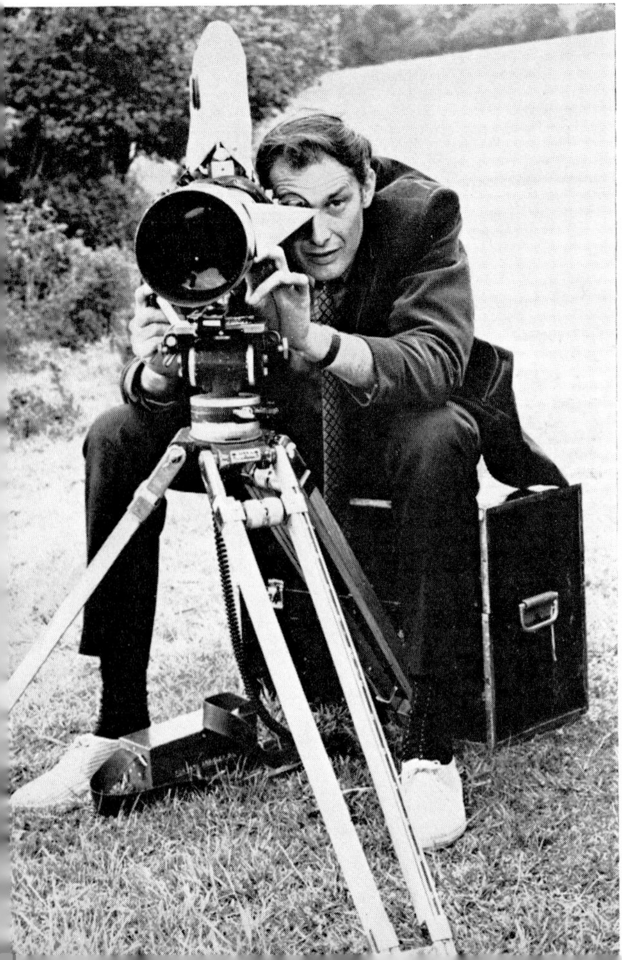

Page 36
(*above*) A rare problem in making wildlife movies; (*left*) using a cardboard sight mounted on a telephoto lens. This is invaluable for finding subjects, such as birds in flight, when at great range.

The framework for this hide (Fig 4) consists of four wooden or light metal uprights which are driven into the ground at the corners of a 3ft square. These should be about 5ft 9in long and the top 1½in of each should be of reduced diameter (if they are made of wood, metal rods can be fixed

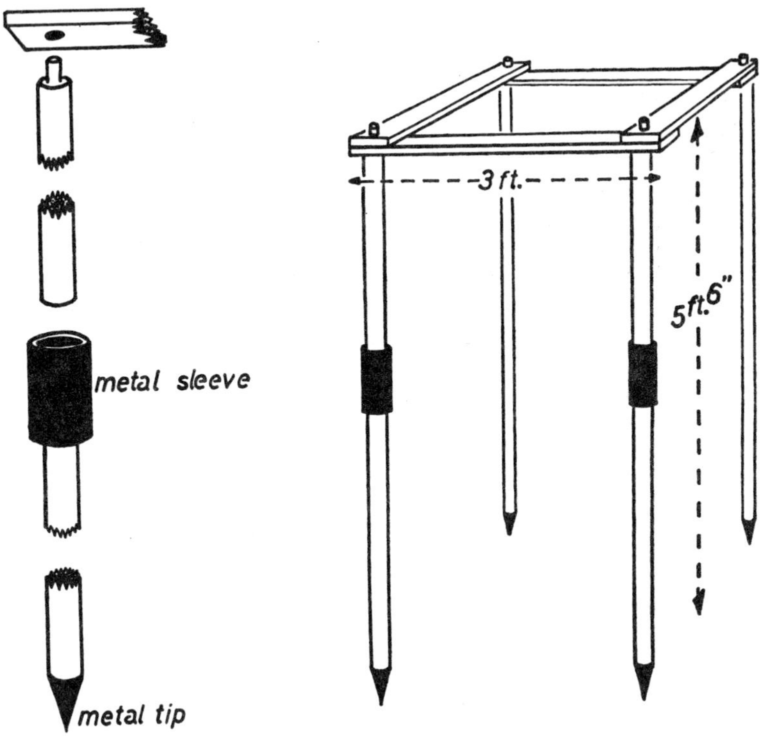

Fig 4 Design for a hide frame

into them at this point) to provide a resting place for four wooden strips each 3ft 1in long with holes 1in from each end. These strips provide a frame for the roof and hold the uprights in the correct position.

To make the hide easy to carry around, each upright should be constructed in two equal detachable sections joined by a metal sleeve. The end that is to be driven into the ground can be sheathed in a metal cone, like a tent pole.

The hide can now be erected, but as yet no provision has been made for a lens hole or for any observation slits. Some hides have elaborate systems of slits with zips on three sides, but my experience has been that however many slits a hide is provided with, there is never one in just the right place for the job. It is usually best to make slits on site, exactly where they are needed, and if they are cut carefully they can always be sewn up again afterwards.

It may also be necessary to make an additional slit for one or two of the tripod legs, and this will depend on camera design and length of lens. With a 16mm camera and a long-focus lens, all three legs can sometimes be accommodated inside the hide, but with an 8mm camera and fairly short lenses a different arrangement will be necessary (Fig 5).

Another complication may arise if the front of the camera has a built-in exposure meter which does not work through the lens. It is as important for this to 'see out' as for the lens,

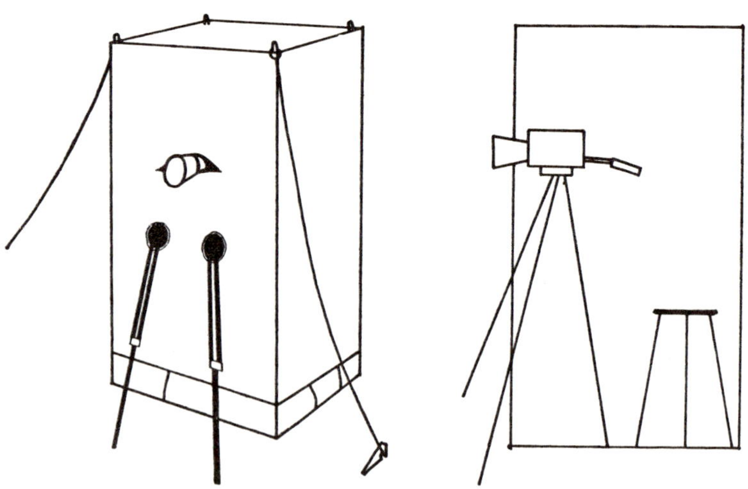

Fig 5 Tripod arrangement for 8mm camera in hide

unless this automatic control is being manually overridden. To accommodate the meter a larger-than-usual slit must be cut in the hide, and two extra cuts made so that a flap of the material can be pinned back and fastened with a safety pin. This will allow adequate panning movement, but in order to camouflage the exposed area of camera it will be necessary to fit a cardboard mask over the lens, leaving a hole for the light cell, and sometimes for a tube from the cell to this mask (Fig 6). The cardboard should be painted the same dark brown or green as the hide material.

NOTEBOOK, PENCIL AND IDENTIFICATION NUMBERS

Most naturalists carry a notebook and pencil around with them as a matter of course, and it is particularly important to have them handy when filming wildlife. Whenever possible, it is well worth noting down after every shot details of the location, species, sex, and anything of interest about the animal's behaviour. You may *think* you will remember this when the film is viewed, but it is always safer to have it written down. Your notes will in any case be very helpful when it comes to the editing stage, especially if this is to be done on an animated viewer with a tiny screen.

You should also record details of technical matters such as exposure, filters, and so on. If any faults are found in the film after processing, this information will help to pin down the trouble.

In ideal circumstances not only should the start of each roll of film be identified with a filmed number, but each shot as well. The latter is usually not possible for most nature work, especially when filming from a hide, so notebook information becomes even more valuable. However, most rolls can be identified by shooting a few frames before entering the hide, and if a new roll is started while in the hide then the

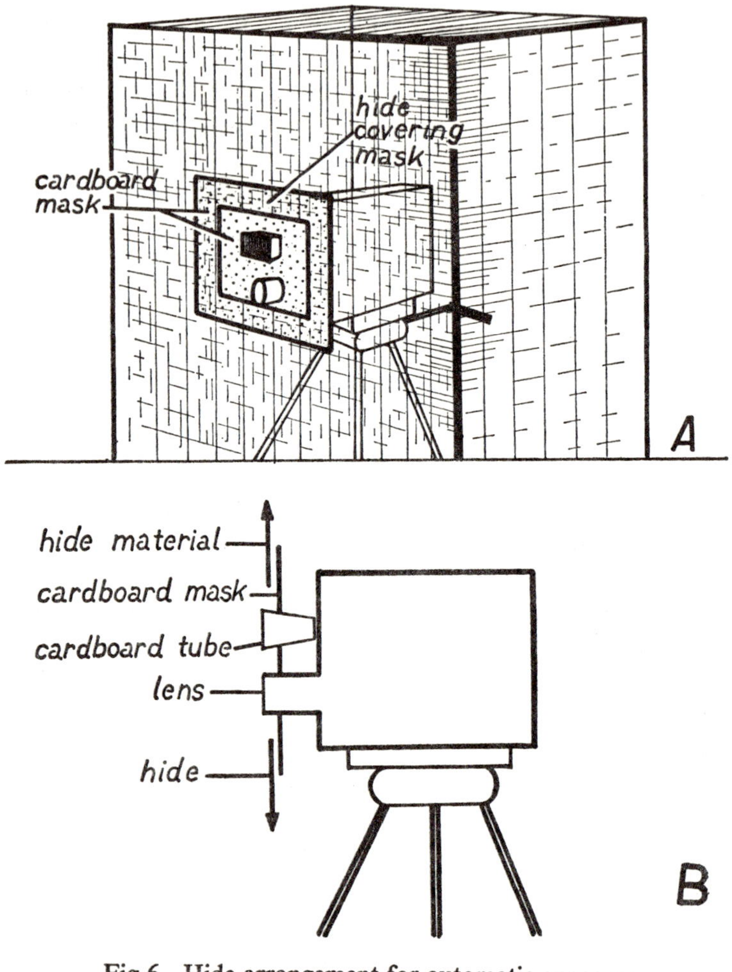

Fig 6 Hide arrangement for automatic exposure control that does not work through the taking lens

appropriate number can be filmed in the middle of the roll after leaving. Professionally, this identification is done by writing in chalk on a small blackboard, but an easier method for the amateur is to film numbers from a small book of cloakroom tickets. These can easily be carried in the pocket, and provided you make a point of tearing out tickets immediately after use there is little risk of using the same number twice.

3

Film, Lights and Exposure

THE choice of film stock for natural history subjects is dominated by one factor: the speed of the film. Indeed, if wild animals are to be filmed in Britain, or if a sequence is to be shot in dense woodland or jungle, all other considerations may have to be ignored. If birds are the film subject, however, then the choice is usually wider.

RANGE OF FILM STOCK

Unhappily, the 8mm enthusiasts do not have a great range of film stock at their disposal. Kodachrome II, Agfacolor and Perutz all have the same speed in daylight, which is 25ASA; and in artificial light, 40ASA.

As 16mm is a professional as well as an amateur gauge there is a good range of black-and-white and colour stock of various speeds. Quite apart from personal whims about the dyes in different colour films, the final choice in this gauge must be influenced by yet another factor: the purpose to which the film is to be put. Kodachrome II and Agfacolor are reversal films, which when exposed and processed are used for direct projection. Since the camera original will be screened over and over again, great care must be taken with it, especially in the editing stages, otherwise the film may bear permanent scratches.

If the film is likely to have many projections and more than one copy is required, the choice of stock lies between a master reversal film such as Ektachrome, or a negative-positive process such as Eastmancolor. Although Ektachrome Commercial Type 7252 is slow (16ASA in daylight with its daylight correction filter) it has a fair exposure latitude and gives really excellent prints of high quality. Personally I find its flesh tones unsatisfactory, but it gives beautiful results on colourful insect and aquarium subjects. If extra speed is required, there is Ektachrome EF Type 7241 (160ASA for daylight work) and Ektachrome Type 7242 (125ASA for artificial light).

Eastmancolor negative is very widely used for all television purposes, and most wildlife films specially shot for television are made on this stock at present. Where there are sequences involving human activities the film gives very faithful flesh tones, and its soft pastel colours are especially good on 'mood' sequences such as early morning mist scenes. The speed of Type 7254 is rated at 64ASA in daylight, using a Wratten filter, but some cameramen expose at 80ASA and even 100ASA in favourable conditions. In an emergency it can be force-processed one or two stops, but with an increase in grain. Exposure latitude is good, and a welcome amount of colour control is possible at the printing stage.

The cost of processing the original is included in the purchase price in the case of amateur stocks like Kodachrome II, but this is not the case with professional stocks such as Ektachrome and Eastmancolor. Moreover, with these one must have a work print in order to be able to see and edit the film, so it is usually desirable to have some financial backing from a natural history society or a television organization.

PROBLEMS OF COLOUR TEMPERATURE

Artificial illumination is only required for a small proportion of wildlife filming, but there are certain sequences which are impossible without it.

Lights are needed (a) when they effectively provide the sole source of illumination in a small area, as for the macro-photography of insects, and (b) where they boost available daylight in a restricted and dark area, as for instance in the filming of a swallow's nest in an old barn.

In both the above cases the total requirements do not usually exceed two 500W 240V lamps on the British electrical system, but there are one or two associated technical snags that must be borne in mind. These stem from the fact that the artificial light emitted from lamps is of a different quality from daylight. Daylight itself varies a good deal more than most people realize, though everybody must have noticed at one time or another how red the light can be at sunrise and sunset. The light from electric lamps also has a lot of light from the red end of the spectrum: we say it is 'warmer' than daylight.

Unless we are careful about the light we use for filming, the colours on the film will look very strange. Quality of light is measured on a colour-temperature scale in degrees Kelvin, and for photographic purposes artificial light with a colour temperature of 3,200K (as opposed to daylight, which is 5,600K) is normally used. The film used should be balanced for the particular colour temperature, and if it is not then an appropriate correction filter must be used to compensate. It must be remembered, however, that when a filter is used the effective speed of the film is reduced.

Let us suppose that the first part of a roll of Ektachrome is used to film caterpillars indoors under lights of 3,200K. No filter is required in the camera as Ektachrome is an artificial-light stock balanced for that particular colour temperature. The second part of the roll is then used to film establishing scenes out of doors. A correction filter for daylight must now be used (Wratten 85) to reduce the light from the blue end of the spectrum. But since less light is now reaching the film emulsion, the effective speed is reduced from

25ASA to 16ASA. In many modern cameras, particularly Super 8, a correction filter is built in and just needs the flick of a switch when changing from conditions of artificial light to daylight.

In a situation in which there is some available daylight but additional artificial light is necessary, there can be an unfortunate mixture of lights of different quality. Usually there are only two ways of dealing with this problem. The first is to see if it is possible to remove the daylight entirely and work with artificial light alone; but unless this is done efficiently and all shafts of daylight are excluded, ugly blue streaks may mar the picture when seen on projection. The second method is to raise the colour temperature of the lights to match the daylight, which can be done by placing blue gelatine filters in front of the lamps. The disadvantage of this is that their effective brightness is reduced and, what is more, a correction filter must be used in the camera with artificial-light stock, so that the film speed is reduced again. Whenever possible, therefore, it is better to follow the first method and try to work with artificial lights alone.

My most memorable encounter with mixed light sources was during the production of a film about Peter Scott, eminent in so many fields but above all as an artist and authority on birds. A large section of the film had to be shot in Scott's studio at Slimbridge in Gloucestershire, and several scenes had his now-famous picture window in the background. To have excluded daylight, in this case, would have defeated the whole object of the exercise, but additional lighting was certainly necessary to photograph Scott at work in close-up against this very light background. In such circumstances my lighting cameraman would normally have used a third solution to this mixed-light problem by covering all windows with orange gelatine, which effectively reduces the colour temperature of incoming daylight to that of the lights. To all intents and purposes this produces an artificial light set-up and the film may be exposed without any correction filter for daylight.

Unfortunately this method could not be used at Slimbridge, partly because gelatines were not available in the size required for the picture window, and partly because they would have had to be fixed on the outside of the windows and this would have disturbed the wild birds a short distance away. So the only solution was to use a very large amount of lighting and to put blue gelatines over the lamps. The result was a studio cluttered with lamp stands in a tangle of cables, except for the small area where Scott was working at his easel. To his credit he remained calmly talking and painting through two long days, managing to look cool though he could not possibly have felt it.

EXPOSURE CONTROL

Many of the Super 8 and some 16mm cameras have automatic through-the-lens exposure control. Although some professionals scorn this as a gimmick designed to take all the art out of photography, there is no doubt that it has advantages for the wildlife cameraman. It is especially useful when working from a hide.

When working in a restricted and dark area with only a couple of peep-holes, it is easy to underestimate a change in light conditions, and in any case impracticable to step outside and take a proper check with a meter. An automatic exposure control in these circumstances can save a good deal of film that might otherwise be wasted.

Automatic exposure control must, however, be used with care, and it is often essential to be able to override the control and operate it manually. Imagine, for example, that a hide has been set up a short distance away from some dense undergrowth at the edge of a wood. Although the general scene is lit only by dappled sunlight, there is a bird's nest in the centre of it which for an hour or so is in full sunlight. Fully zoomed in, the camera lens sees the bird and nest in full frame and the exposure is automatically and correctly given by the camera. If the lens is then zoomed back to a wide angle, the automatic exposure control starts to compensate for the dominant dark green and half-lit foliage. The bird, which may still be the real camera subject, is then overexposed and the colours of its plumage will be washed out.

There are two possible ways of arriving at a correct exposure with the aid of a conventional separate meter when working from a hide. A reflected light reading can be taken through the front, or, if this is likely to disturb the camera subject, an incident light reading can be taken from the back of the hide by easing the flap a little. Of course, if the hide is situated in the middle of a colony just as much disturbance can be caused by movement at the back as at the front!

4

Birds at the Nest

WHEN, many years ago, I joined the staff of the British Broadcasting Corporation, I very soon found myself editing film sequences for a new natural history programme. Each edition was introduced by Peter Scott in the Bristol television studio, from a set which was supposed to depict a part of his real studio at his Slimbridge bird sanctuary. The atmosphere was always informal, and there was usually a guest naturalist-cameraman present who was responsible for the film to be shown in that particular edition.

Quite often these early television film sequences were re-edited and shortened versions of longer lecture films that had previously been shown to natural history societies. My task was to help select the most suitable sequences and to try to polish up the editing for television presentation. The film available at that time was dominated by sequences of birds at the nest, and by the end of my first year's work I would leap with joy in the cutting-room if I discovered even a short section of film showing a bird doing something other than incubate its eggs or feed its young.

At first I thought the reason for this surfeit of breeding birds was, quite simply, that it was easiest to film a bird at the nest. I discovered subsequently that this was only a half-truth and that in fact the nest provided the best situation for a good 'still' portrait. Most of the cameramen whose film we were using were excellent still-photographers who had moved over to cine work without realizing that a film is a good deal more than a succession of animated photographs. They had not yet begun to exploit to the full the possibilities of the cine camera.

In all fairness, it must be admitted that these early films, out of which the natural history programmes of modern television grew, had satisfied the audience for which they were originally intended. A captive audience of naturalists would have been perfectly happy to watch a series of good bird colour photographs accompanied by an interesting commentary, let alone *moving* pictures of the same birds.

When it came to making television versions of these films, there were other things to be considered. Firstly, we were working in black and white, and a kingfisher or a bee-eater without its colours is less than half the bird. Many scenes at once became devalued, and others had to be rejected or shortened. Secondly, the audience was totally different. Although it was captive in one sense, we were attempting to interest a wide range of people, few of whom would ever have taken the trouble to go to a lecture hall. But such was the fascination of natural history on television that at first we found it possible to hold a large audience on twenty minutes of birds at the nest, provided we did not dwell too long on any one species. This state of affairs soon came to an end, however, for as soon as examples of all the main groups of birds had been seen, this sort of film material began to have an all-too-familiar look about it. To most laymen a purple heron filmed at its nest in the Camargue looks just the same as one filmed in the Spanish Coto Donana; and the behaviour of a common tern at the nest is not vastly different from that of a little tern. Fortunately, before there was any real danger of people becoming bored with the same old birds at different nests, a new and talented race of wildlife cameramen began to appear.

Today, a film featuring nothing but the nesting behaviour

of birds would be the exception rather than the rule. Nevertheless, sequences at the nest do have an important place in many wildlife films, so long as it is realized that once a hide has been set up near a nest there is rather more to do than just to take a couple of shots of the bird settling on her eggs. Here is a list of interesting sequences for filming:

1 construction of the nest
2 courtship and mating
3 behaviour of adults during incubation, including change-over when both sexes incubate
4 hatching of eggs, removal of shells from nest
5 adults feeding young, removing faecal sacs
6 development of young: stages in growth of feathers, young exercising wings, leaving nest
7 territorial behaviour between adjacent pairs in the case of colonial species
8 action of predators on eggs or young

SETTING UP A HIDE

The task of finding the right nest and setting up a hide in a suitable filming position without disturbance to the birds can take just as much time as the actual photography. The beginner would do well to set up his first hide at a nest fairly close to the ground—preferably in his own garden or in the immediate vicinity of his home where he is acquainted with the landowners. Further afield he can do no better than take a leaf out of the professional wildlife cameraman's book, who usually gets a local ornithologist to tell him where the birds are and introduce him to the farmer or landowner concerned. What saves time for the professional is useful also for the amateur who has to cram his filming into a long weekend or a week's holiday.

When a suitable nest has been located, the position of the hide can be decided upon in relation to the various relevant factors, such as the height of the nest, the amount of cover round it, the position of the sun and the kind of lenses available. The more advanced incubation is, the less the danger that the birds will desert, but generally speaking the *final* position of the hide should not be less than 5ft from the nest in the case of a small bird such as a wren or a warbler, and 10ft in the case of a ground-nesting bird such as a lapwing. The word 'final' is stressed, because if nest-desertion is to be avoided the hide should first be erected several yards away and then gradually worked in (Fig 7). This may not be possible because of the geography of the area or because of trees and bushes in the way, in which case the hide should be placed in the final filming position, but assembled in three or four stages over several days (Fig 8). In fact, it is desirable to erect the hide in stages even if one starts some distance away.

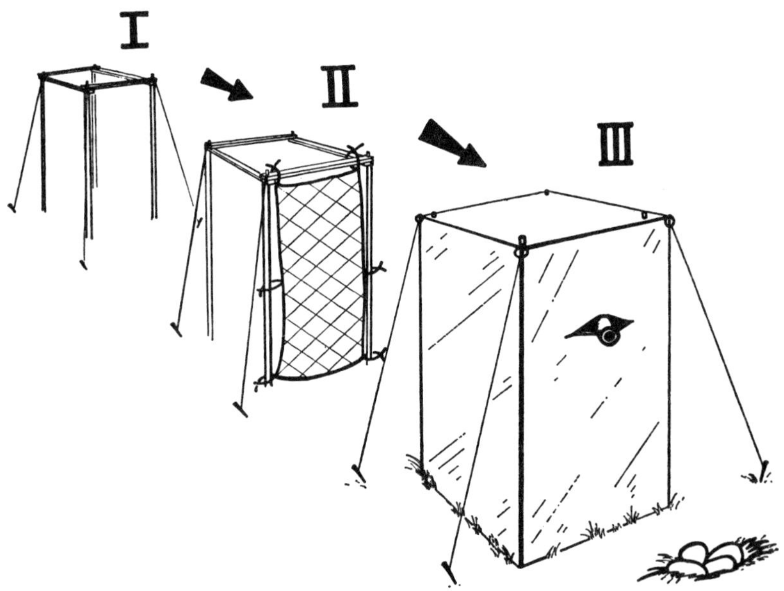

Fig 7 Stages in the erection of a hide for ground-nesting birds

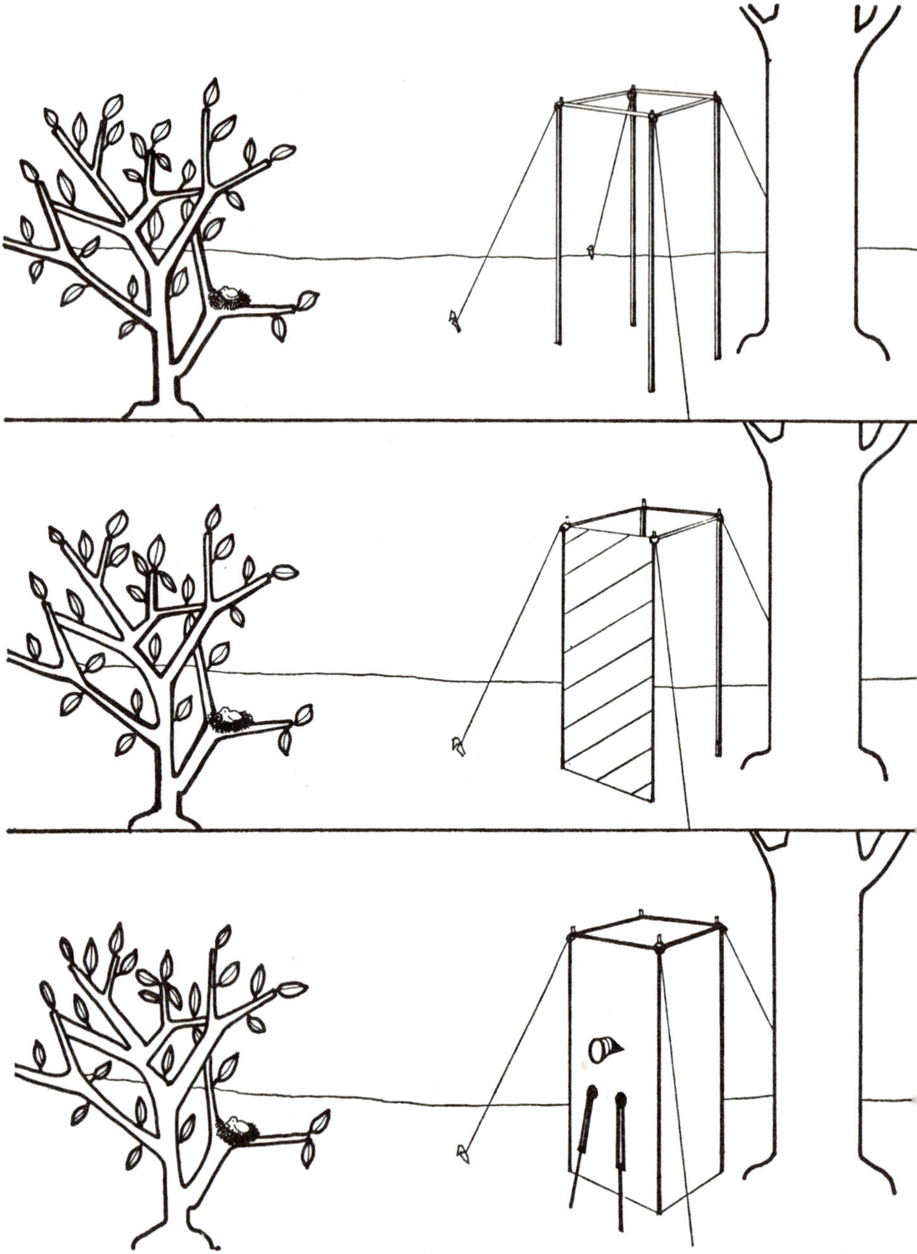

Fig 8 Stages in the erection of a hide when only one position is possible

On the first visit to the nest, the hide framework only should be placed in position, with possibly a piece of old sacking tied across the roof. Everything should be secure, the sacking should not flap, and the uprights should be held down firmly with guy-ropes. Provided as short a time as possible is spent in setting up the hide, the operation should not cause alarm to the birds. The following day the temporary hide may be moved in a little closer and another piece of sacking, or material similar to the covering of the hide, should be tied to the front two supports; this again should be secure enough not to flap about in the wind. After yet another day the whole hide may be put up in its final position. After each stage in the erecting of the hide it is advisable to retreat some distance and observe the bird's return to the nest through field-glasses. If on any occasion the bird fails to return, that stage should be modified immediately and the hide moved back or the cover removed.

Because many birds like to tuck their nests away in cover it may be necessary to rearrange some of the surrounding plant and tree growth, in order to avoid having untidy out-of-focus foliage in shot. The word 'rearrange' is used deliberately, because there have been some appalling examples of what is known in the business as 'gardening'. I recall one sequence of a blackcap at the nest, in which the bird was seen through a neat port-hole where pruning shears had been used to cut an observation window through to the nest. In another case, this time a ground-nesting bird, the foreground grass had been carefully cut short with shears. Quite apart from the increased danger of predator disturbance, the scenes that result from this sort of treatment look quite unnatural.

The hide position should already give the best possible view of the nest, but the first look through the camera viewfinder may reveal some obstruction. Usually, however, the actual nest is only partially obscured by two or three twigs or a few blades of grass. In the case of the latter, just a *few* of the offending ones may be cut very close to the ground; as for the twigs, these can be rearranged by holding them out of shot with fine dark thread. After filming has been completed, the thread is cut and everything falls back into place again.

Provided that the hide walls and roof are in brown and green colours that tone well with the surrounding countryside, further camouflage of branches, dry grass and other material is unnecessary as far as the birds are concerned. It is, however, highly desirable to reduce the risk of human interference, both on the cameraman's and on the birds' account: the very presence of a hide automatically pin-points a nest. One might hope that people seeing a hide would assume that it was being used for photography and keep well away. It is not unknown, however, for a local inhabitant to stroll up to the front of an occupied hide, peer down the lens, and breezily pass the time of day. Needless to say, this kind of incident usually occurs at particularly inopportune moments, just as something interesting begins to happen. So if the hide is within sight of a road or lane or a regularly used path, it should be made as inconspicuous as possible by decorating the outside with whatever is growing immediately around it.

The most conspicuous hides of all are those erected to photograph ground-nesting birds such as curlews and meadow pipits. Here there is little point in even trying to make the hide merge with its surroundings, for whatever you do the thing will almost invariably stand out like a sore thumb. You can only hope that the situation is remote enough for human interference to be unlikely. Human beings are not the only enemy. Cows, too, are very inquisitive, and it is only a matter of time before hooved animals in the vicinity take advantage of the hide as a convenient scratching or rubbing post. This can be distressing – whether the cameraman happens to be in the hide at the time or whether he arrives next morning to find a crumpled heap of wood and fabric. The only practical way of preventing this sort of disaster is to surround the hide with a couple of strands of barbed wire fixed on four posts. Once again, if the hide is to be set up on farmland, the co-operation of the farmer should be enlisted.

When filming at a nest, the lens of the camera should always be at a greater height than the rim of the nest. Not only does this give satisfactory views of the eggs and nestlings, but the round shape of the nest improves the composition. Nests more than four feet from the ground, therefore, nearly always have to be filmed from hides built on platforms – not an exercise for beginners. The erection of such platforms when needed will obviously then become the first stage in the preliminary hide-erection routine already discussed. They can be mounted on stout stakes driven into the ground, or set up on tall 'pylon' structures, or even built on poles lashed to the branches of trees. Whichever system of construction is used, stability is the important thing to remember.

If a cameraman is working with a long telephoto lens, the slightest vibration travelling up through the tripod legs results in picture unsteadiness, which can easily render the film useless. It is clear then that the higher up a tree the hide is situated, the greater the movements caused by winds and the more acute the problem for the photographer. When filming crows, rooks, herons and other birds that nest high up it is preferable to build the hide in the same tree as the nest, provided of course that the tree is large enough. The hide and nest are then more likely to sway in sympathy with one another as the whole tree moves in the wind, and therefore the position of the hide in relation to the nest will remain reasonably constant. Nevertheless, it is not advisable to attempt this sort of work in anything more than a light breeze.

GETTING DOWN TO WORK

When filming nesting birds from a hide it is essential to have an assistant. An extra pair of hands is very useful to help carry all the camera equipment, a stool, sandwiches, thermos flask and so on. Most important of all, however, is that someone must be seen to *leave* the hide before the bird will normally return.

Though the incubating bird will have flown away as an approach is made to the nest, it is quite likely that it will be only at a short distance, anxious to return and keeping a wary eye on the situation. If this is the case, then someone walking away from the hide will lead the bird to accept that the danger is over.

To complete the illusion, it is also important that someone should relieve the cameraman when he has finished his work. Giving a definite time for this is not a good idea, for the arrival of the assistant might coincide with some particularly interesting behaviour at the nest. A clearly visible pre-arranged signal can be used to indicate that the cameraman has finished filming: the hanging of a white handkerchief outside the *back* of the hide, for instance.

Two, or if at all possible, three different lenses should be used when filming activities at the nest: one to give a wide establishing scene in which the nest may be only $\frac{1}{6}$ or $\frac{1}{8}$ of frame size; another to give medium close shots in which the bird and nest fit comfortably into the frame with room to spare; and a third to provide big close-ups showing rather less than half the bird.

The first wide-angle scene establishes the nest site, but it will be visually uninteresting if the bird is already sitting on the nest. It is better to wait until the bird returns to the nest, either to incubate or feed the young, and then the action of the bird approaching, perhaps hopping from twig to twig, will not only provide interest but will lead the eye automatically to the nest, which with this lens may be rather difficult to see. In order to provide enough material for editing, it is recommended that at least two such shots are filmed for each sex when a detailed feeding or incubating sequence is being built up.

Medium close shots will probably add up to 60 or 70 per cent of the total film. In good length takes these will show most activities, such as settling down to incubate and feeding the young. But editing will be easier if a few big close-ups are also filmed in addition to the wider scenes already mentioned. Used sparingly, big close-ups will enrich the sequence quite dramatically. Even when the bird is incubating and quite still a close-up can show a particularly attractive part of the bird's head plumage, or perhaps the use of the nictitating membrane over the eye. The value of the occasional big close-up to enable medium shots to be edited together cannot be stressed too strongly.

In a nest sequence it is difficult to obtain big close-ups of the adult birds in any position other than at the nest itself, because of their constant movement on approach and departure. However, a study of the birds' routes to the nest will reveal a number of well-used intermediate perches as they make their way in. By focusing on one of these and watching through a peep-hole, the camera can be started just before the bird flies on to the perch, and this additional close-up will supply some useful extra seconds when the sequence is edited. If there are no suitable perches within good camera range, it is often possible to arrange one on the bird's route.

This trick can be particularly useful with a bird such as the kingfisher, which has the annoying habit of zooming upstream like a blue flash and diving into its nest-hole in the bank before as much as a second or two of film has gone through the camera.

FILMING NEST CONSTRUCTION

Film sequences of nest construction have been neglected by most professionals and also by the dedicated band of semi-professionals who shoot so much film for television. This may be because there is a great danger of the birds deserting at this stage. However, a few very successful sequences have been taken, as in Christopher Mylne's excellent films of swallows and reed warblers made for the British Royal Society for the Protection of Birds, but there is plenty of scope for new work in this field.

Swallows, and perhaps to an even greater extent house martins, provide some of the best opportunities. As the birds return to the same nest sites year after year, plans for filming them can be made even before they arrive. Swallows build inside outhouses and barns, and this means that there are problems with lighting. There is usually enough daylight coming in through a window to watch the birds but not enough to film them by, so lamps have to be used. Fortunately most farms now have an electricity supply, and an arrangement could probably be made with the farmer for the use of current.

Conditioning birds to artificial lighting has to be tackled in much the same way as conditioning them to a hide. Assuming that the final illumination will be provided by two 500W photo-floods a few feet away from the nest, operations should commence with the lights several yards away at considerably less power than 500W – say at 25W. If nest-building is to be filmed, then this stage must be carried out after the birds have arrived but before nesting operations have begun. All moves must be made very cautiously, since the birds may choose some other nesting place if everything is not in their favour. It is as well to try to prevent this by arranging for other barn and outhouse doors and windows to remain closed.

All subsequent repositioning of lamps and increase in illumination must be guided by the birds' reaction to the first stage. The lights should be moved in as quickly as possible when building begins, yet rushing things may make the birds leave. The more accustomed the birds are to human activity around the farm, the easier will be the task.

The filming of swallows at the nest provides a classic situation where there are two light sources of different colour temperature. This problem has already been discussed in Chapter 3. If insufficient illumination results from placing blue gelatines over the lamps and shooting for daylight, there is no alternative but to try to minimize the incoming daylight and shoot in artificial light. Obviously one cannot exclude daylight altogether if the swallows are to have means of access to the barn, but by angling the barn windows or by tying up a black masking sheet one can sometimes avoid any direct fall of daylight onto the nest area.

House martins present fewer problems than swallows because they build under the eaves on the outside of buildings. Also, their nests are often quite close together, which gives a useful choice of subject from one camera position. Even on a sunny day the nests are nearly always in deep shadow, so particular care must be taken in focusing, as the lens aperture will be rather wide and there will be little depth of field. To obtain satisfactory matching scenes, it is best to film the wider shots of the birds flying to and from the nest-site on a bright but cloudy day; otherwise, if exposure is made for sunlit areas, the nests in shadow will be practically invisible.

Swallows and house martins both provide particularly good opportunities for nest-building sequences because one can usually trace the location from which they are collecting mud. This may be the bank of a stream or pond, or a muddy puddle on a track a few hundred yards away, and once it has been found, a hide can be erected quite quickly since the area will almost invariably be one in which the birds are used to a certain amount of intermittent disturbance. Indeed, if long lenses are available, it is often possible to film mud-collecting without a hide, or better still from the back of a van or car. These scenes will provide excellent intercuts with the actual nest construction and make a big contribution to the visual appeal of the sequence as a whole.

The collecting of nest material in other species is considerably more difficult to film, though birds using the garden provide some scope. I have found that birds engaged on building nests will collect grasses, hair and feathers placed on a lawn, provided that these are reasonably conspicuous and are within the territory of the birds in question.

NESTS IN HOLES AND BURROWS

Filming inside a tree or in an underground burrow is just about the most difficult work possible at the nest, and quite understandably the occasions when it has been pulled off successfully are rare. Film work of this kind is not for the one-day-a-week cameraman, for not only does it require a great deal of preparation but also extremely close observation of the nesting bird's behaviour, so that filming can be suspended at once if it becomes unduly alarmed and seems likely to desert. Anyone with any illusions about the time and effort involved in such filming should read Rosemary Eastman's *The Kingfisher* and, if possible, Heinz Sielmann's *My Year with the Woodpeckers* (at present, 1970, out of print).

Broadly speaking, there are two general methods for tackling the problem, and unless the nest site is on your own property both need the full co-operation of the landowner. The first method is to wait until the bird is already established with eggs inside its nesting-hole, and then very carefully tunnel or bore alongside it until the nest chamber is reached. This is a very time-consuming operation and is made more so by the fact that it can only be done in short periods at a time. It is unlikely that the bird will remain incubating whilst it is going on, and the eggs must not be allowed to get cold.

Simultaneously with the tunnelling work, a hide is built, in stages, so that by the time the nest chamber is reached the hide is complete. In the case of birds nesting in tree-holes, the hide can either be on a pylon structure next to the tree, or be actually fixed to the same tree.

The method used by Ronald and Rosemary Eastman when filming kingfishers and starlings was to construct a hide several feet from the nest chamber and connect the two by a funnel. This funnel, which was nearly 3ft wide at the hide end, also housed the two internal reflector 375W lamps.

The really critical point comes just before the nest chamber is broken into. There is a great danger that earth or wood may fall in on top of the eggs, so it is usual to remove them and keep them warm (direct handling should be avoided or the bird may not return to incubate). A piece of framed glass is then fixed against the side of the nest chamber, and made secure. The eggs are replaced, and the outside of the glass is covered up by replacing a section of wood over it, or a screen of some sort in the case of an underground burrow.

The nest chamber is then still in total darkness and there is a very tense moment while it is seen whether or not the incubating bird will accept the glass. The chances are good, provided it does not intrude too far into the nest area. Then the next stage of the preparations for filming can be started, and that is conditioning the incubating bird to accept lights. By this time, of course, an electricity supply must be made available, on site. In remote areas a generator has to be hired and parked some distance away where the sound of its engine will not affect the birds.

Once inside the darkness of the hide, the cameraman carefully uncovers the glass window, and when the adult bird has returned and settled, he carefully turns on the first very low-power lamp. Ideally, this should be on a fader so that the light level can be raised very slowly, otherwise a whole succession of lamps of increasing power should be used until the incubating bird does not mind even full illumination being turned on. It should be noted that the birds cannot be conditioned to *permanent* lighting because the heat would quickly cause distress. Strobe lighting devices (see page 112), though at present usually too expensive for the amateur, provide the best solution to the heat/light problem.

The second method for obtaining nest-chamber sequences can be adopted where birds are known to return to the same nest sites year after year. Then all the preparations with glass window and the associated hide can be made at leisure before the breeding season, perhaps even before the birds return to the country in the case of migrants.

This is surely the method to be preferred, for it involves hardly any risk to the breeding birds, though it does mean that the cameraman has to take a gamble. The year that he decides to embark on all these elaborate preparations could be just the very year that the birds decide to move elsewhere, and leave him with an empty nest and a useless hide.

The risk of the nest chamber remaining empty can be minimized, first by making the hide as neat as possible, with no interference to the nest entrance, and then by making sure that the nest is still the most attractive choice in the area for that particular species. This calls for observation and some research into the preferences of the birds. If, for example, one species seems to prefer holes with a convenient perch nearby, the chosen site should be checked to see if one exists already; if not, a suitable perch can be planted. At the same time the attractions of other sites in the neighbourhood can be reduced by removing perches that might be favoured by prospecting birds.

When filming kingfishers underground, Ronald Eastman used an extremely elegant combination of these two main principles. In an area in which there were only rather stony banks, he installed an artificial but ideal nesting bank in which the birds could easily dig a burrow. At the same time the rear of this bank was made accessible for filming. After a pair of kingfishers had in fact started digging, Eastman waited until he felt sure that the birds had practically completed their excavations, then he started boring in from the rear until he nearly, but not quite, met the kingfishers' burrow. There he inserted a piece of board, with a frame at his side of it ready to take a suitable piece of glass. The kingfishers, which were by then nearing completion of their digging in any case, reached the impenetrable board and immediately made their nesting chamber, exactly in the right place for Eastman's filming window.

FILMING IN COLONIES

Rewarding hours can be spent in a hide placed in the middle of a colony of nesting birds such as gulls or terns. In this case it is desirable to be able to film from three sides of the hide as there may be several nest sites round about, and all within a few feet of each other. Not only are there then more nests to choose from, but there is also a greater range of behaviour to film: courtship, mating, nest-building and feeding, as well as a good deal of inter-territorial behaviour between adjacent nests. Once the young have hatched there is a good chance of them wandering off and getting into trouble with their neighbours. With all this activity there is also a very real danger of extravagant use of film.

When the richness of colony behaviour is filmed and interpreted by an authority like Professor Niko Tinbergen, the result is a masterpiece. His *Signals for Survival*, a film about animal communication in a colony of lesser black-backed gulls, won the Italia Prize (Documentary Section) for the British Broadcasting Corporation in 1969. An extremely complex sound track helped the film on its way, but the success of *Signals for Survival* underlines the importance of the cameraman having a deep understanding of his subject. Many cameramen have shot considerable footage at gull colonies before, much of it very beautiful in photographic terms. Yet Professor Tinbergen's film, although no more than technically very competent, was a classic, for under the direction of Hugh Falkus the camera was made to reveal in a masterly way Tinbergen's interpretation of the complexities of a great bird city. And it showed that in exceptional cases it *is* possible, even today, to hold the viewer's interest at or near the nest not just for twenty minutes but for nearly fifty.

A FINAL WORD

Once filming at the nest has been completed and the hide removed, it is important to take one or two establishing scenes. These may be filmed some distance away from the nest site, but they will prove valuable in showing the surrounding countryside and the habitat in which the nest is situated. They are comparatively simple to film, yet they are frequently forgotten until editing time comes – and then it is too late.

5

Away from the Nest

One of the first men to produce good studies of birds away from the nest was a British naturalist from Norfolk, Dick Bagnall-Oakeley. His work was shown in some early television nature programmes and included fine cine shots of various waders, ducks, waxwings, redwings, fieldfares, bramblings and many other birds, all feeding, flying, swimming, preening or engaged in activities other than nesting.

For most of the time Bagnall-Oakeley dispensed with a hide and stalked his film subjects. His Bolex camera was fitted with a pistol grip, and many of his shots were taken crouched or lying behind the cover of reeds or grasses, with the camera braced, using elbows as supports. Although his shots with telephoto lenses were remarkably steady, this is not a technique that can be generally recommended. Because of the difficulty of holding a steady shot with lenses of very long focal length, birds have to be approached especially close. This means that there is a very real danger of the cameraman being seen, and a watchful bird giving the alarm. The other drawback of this stalking method, of course, is the extreme physical discomfort that is often experienced.

Bearing in mind the freedom of birds and the many places where they can hop, perch, fly, swim and dive, it may seem a formidable task to get near enough to film these activities without stalking. But the problems are nothing like as great as they seem at first. Each species feeds on a certain type of food and therefore in a restricted part of the countryside. For other activities, such as courtship, birds often use the same area, sometimes a very restricted one, every year.

A cameraman has great scope here for opportunist shooting, by which I mean taking advantage of something that turns up whilst he is waiting to film some other activity, and possibly some other species. For example, he may be filming a coot or a moorhen from a hide when a heron flies in and starts fishing in an ideal position. It is sometimes recommended that the cameraman should shoot only what is demanded by the filmscript, but in natural-history work that rule often has to be ignored, otherwise he will miss golden opportunities that might never occur again.

In filming away-from-the-nest activities remember again that if the locality is not a familiar one, then the help of a local ornithologist should be sought. He will be able to pinpoint the feeding-grounds and courtship areas of many species, and save days of hunting about that might otherwise have been spent filming.

ESTUARY FEEDING

From late summer to the end of winter one of the most rewarding habitats in which to film is a river estuary. A large estuary at high tide can look an unpromising film location, but often, as the tide recedes, various small creeks and bays become feeding areas for a variety of species. In one estuary that I know well there is one particular area where the mallard congregate, another preferred by wigeon, a little bay where diving ducks come, a strip of marshy ground frequented by greenshanks, and a patch of mud favoured by the godwit. As soon as a feeding pattern like this has been discovered, the cameraman can begin to look at the filming problems.

Twice daily there is a general movement of birds on

estuaries. As the tide sweeps in, wading birds are pushed closer to the shore, to the point where, if it is a particularly high tide, they may have to fly some distance to find a place to rest. Some of them may move into nearby fields, while the smaller waders like dunlin, sanderling and knot, will probably concentrate in great masses on the last available patch of mud. When the tide recedes, the birds disperse again and gradually return to their favourite feeding-grounds.

In the winter, when filming days are short, estuary photography has to be carefully planned with the aid of a tide-table. To obtain spectacular shots of masses of waders, filming may have to be done at a weekend when there is a good high spring tide around midday. A spring tide at, say, 5 pm might be too late for crowd scenes, but it might provide good filming in one of the feeding areas in early afternoon when the tide is beginning to push some of the birds towards a camera position near the bank.

For filming a concentration of waders at high tide, a hide can be erected just an hour or so before shooting commences. Some of the birds may even be visible a few hundred yards away on the mud while the hide is being put up, but this should make little difference if they are waders. Waders are used to a good deal of human interference, and some of the small ones, like sanderling, are so confiding that they can be filmed on a telephoto lens without a hide. However, the use of a hide enables a greater variety of species to be filmed, and if it is correctly placed some waders will only be a few feet away from it at high tide.

The position of the sun is always important, but in this instance so also is yesterday's high-tide line. Having found that, an adjustment must be made for the change in level of high water, and the best position for the hide assessed; an error in judgement will mean either that the cameraman is too far away from the birds or that he gets his feet wet.

Of the three types of shot – long, medium and close – the

medium shot is least satisfactory with waders unless it is to show a particularly attractive back-lit effect or a comparison between two or three species. Close-ups are needed to show subtle differences in plumage and feeding methods. Long shots give a good impression of numbers and the atmosphere of the estuary; for these, side or back lighting is usually most effective as it brings out patterns of water reflections and mud shapes, which are the essence of estuary atmosphere.

Ducks and geese are usually much more wary than waders and preparations for filming them must be given more care. This is especially true of species like mallard, wigeon and teal, because they are so often targets for guns. For these birds it pays to camouflage the hide by siting it between bushes and covering exposed canvas with branches. A protruding telephoto lens can be disguised by covering it with a sleeve made of dark green material. The long length of black metal, looking rather like a gun barrel, has often been known to make ducks nervous.

Diving birds, like golden-eye and redbreasted merganser, which are often seen in the deeper, more inaccessible water of the estuary, may tempt some cameramen to approach them in a boat hide. Having seen film shot in this way, I would strongly discourage such attempts unless conditions were ideal. A small boat is a highly unstable and most unsatisfactory camera platform unless the camera is hand-held using a wide-angle lens, and this is rarely any use for filming birds. When a telephoto lens is used, a list of even a fraction of a degree can send the framed picture whizzing out of the viewfinder, and the resulting film is almost guaranteed to make the viewer seasick. However, if a hide is set up on the largest boat available and this is anchored in a suitable position on a very calm day, then some success can be had. Extra passengers should be totally discouraged; not only is it difficult to keep them out of sight, but it is highly unlikely that they will be able to sit still for any length of time.

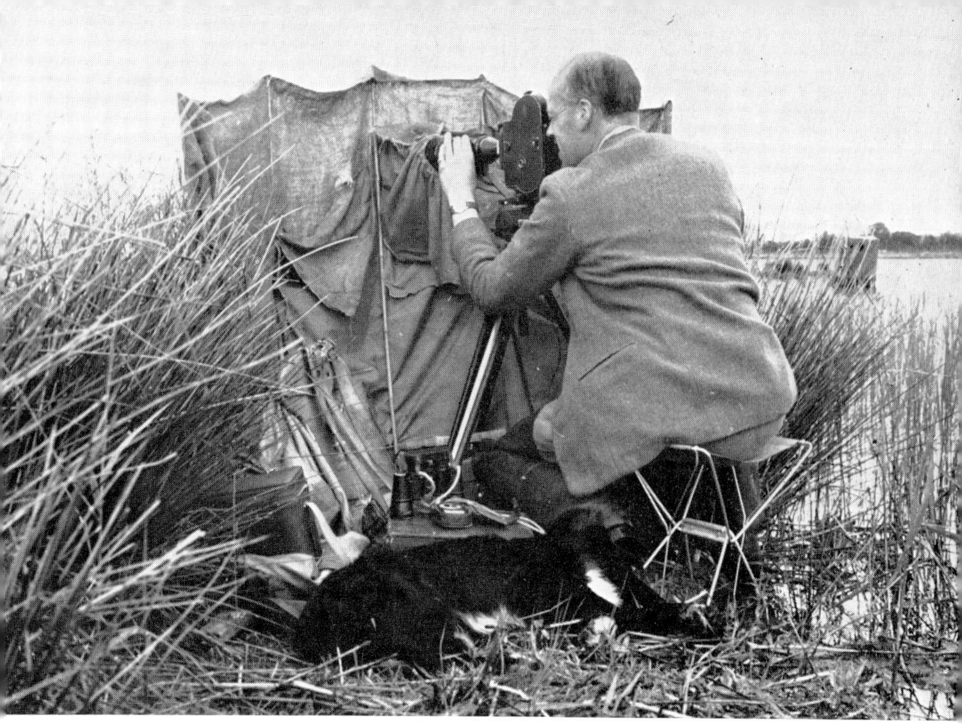

Page 69 (*above*) An unusual open type of hide used by Christopher Mylne for filming the display of great crested grebes. Although it has the advantage of comfort in fine weather, this hide can only be used for birds that will never pass over or behind it; (*below*) two standard hides erected near a stream to film swallows collecting nest mud. Note the barbed wire to keep cattle away.

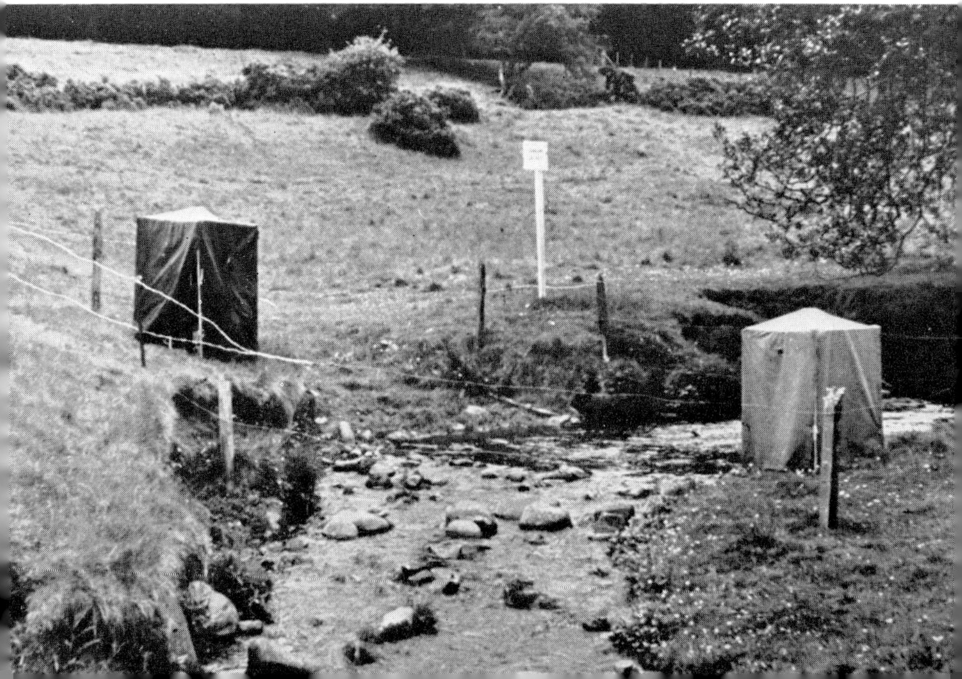

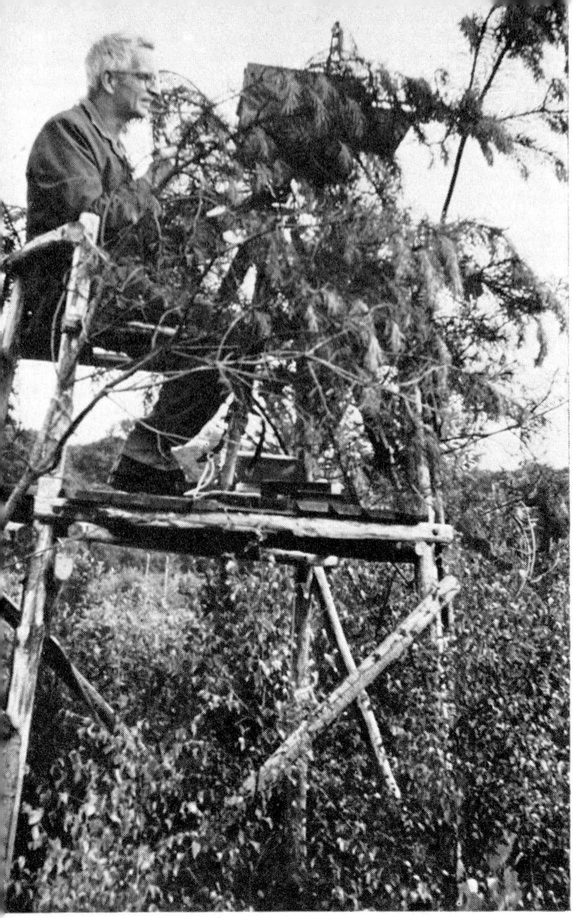

Page 70
(*left*) Filming deer: a high seat, normally used for shooting with a gun rather than with a camera, is used here by Eric Ashby; (*below*) filming badgers: Eric Ashby uses no hide but a few branches and pieces of bracken are used to break up the hard lines of the tripod legs. His own shape is broken up by the tree behind.

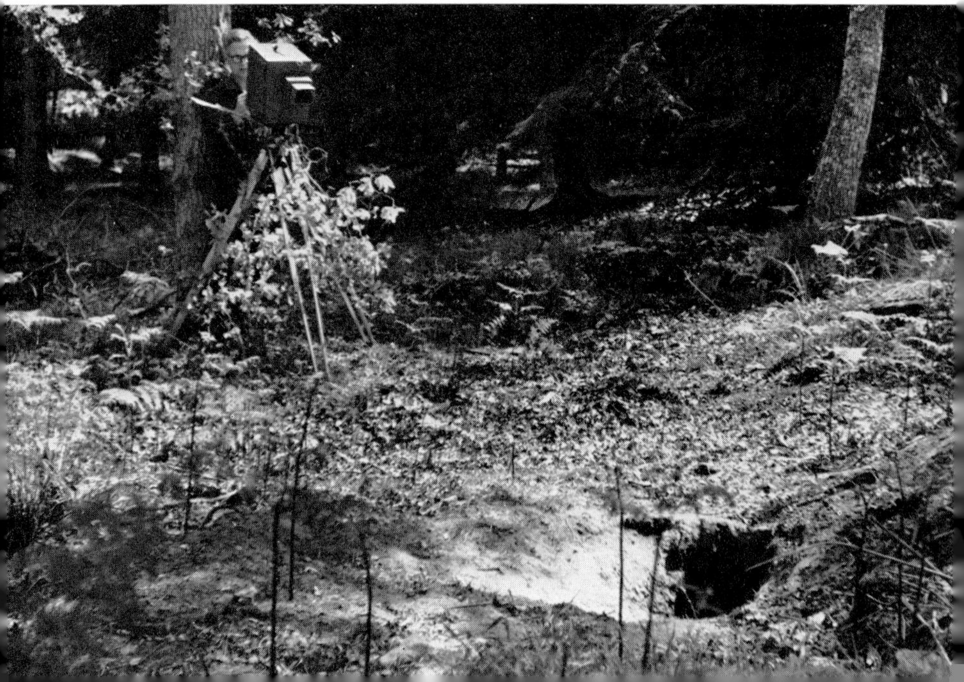

WINTER FEEDING

In addition to wildfowl and waders on estuaries, ponds and reservoirs, there is plenty of scope for filming birds feeding elsewhere in the general countryside in winter. At this time of the year they are much easier to see and to film, and when conditions are hard their hunger makes them tamer. In late autumn it is a good plan to make a note of trees and bushes with good crops of berries, for these will receive a lot of attention from the birds later on. Corn ricks and their immediate surroundings used to be good feeding areas for finches, but with improved farming methods and the use of combine harvesters, such excellent locations have become difficult to find.

As soon as birds start going for the food sources that you have noted then is the time to erect a hide without delay. If the site is by a roadside it is probably best to film from a parked vehicle (see page 79).

BAITING

Sometimes it is possible to make an artificial supply of food available at a convenient camera position. This is called 'baiting', and it is a particularly useful method of filming feeding sequences.

A few years ago I was particularly anxious to film jays taking acorns from an oak tree. When the fruit is ripe jays gorge themselves at the tree and pouch what they cannot eat on the spot. Then they fly away to push the pouched acorns into the ground, presumably as a late winter store. Perhaps they manage to retrieve a few of them in hard times; certainly many of them eventually grow into oak trees.

I required a sequence showing this behaviour for *The Major*, a film about the life of an old oak tree which was used as a village notice-board and meeting-place. The jay shots were particularly important since they were to come immediately before the final tree-felling sequence, to show how the old oak's line would continue through the action of the jays. There were descriptions of this jay behaviour in scientific journals but there was no existing film of it, so Eric Ashby was given the task of recording these scenes on film for the first time. As he lived in the middle of the New Forest, his house and grounds surrounded by oak woods, he at least had some chance of success. Indeed, when the acorns ripened on a tree within a few hundred yards of his home and the jays started moving in, so did Ashby. Using a chicken shed in an adjoining field as a hide, he filmed the first few shots of the jays plucking acorns. Unfortunately it was a very bad year for acorns, and they were all gone before anything like sufficient film had been taken. Other trees nearby had no acorns at all, so things began to look black for our key sequence.

In desperation, Eric Ashby and I drove round the surrounding countryside looking for oak trees with acorns. After several hours' search we arrived back at his house with a collection of branches, some of which we tied onto the tree previously visited by the jays. To our delight back came the jays and started working feverishly. Every time they stripped the branches fresh ones were put up, until the supply was exhausted. When the sequence had been successfully filmed, we realized that we had been fortunate after all in having to work in a bad acorn year; for a shortage of acorns had made the jays return to the one source they knew, and at which they could be conveniently filmed.

Possibly the most ingenious and best-known example of baiting in recent years was that used by Ronald and Rosemary Eastman in their highly successful attempt to film a kingfisher taking its prey from a stream. By making fish readily and regularly available at a tiny artificial pond fitted with special photographic facilities (the whole apparatus being within the confines of the kingfisher's stream), they were able to record the kingfisher's dives both above and under water.

A much less sophisticated form of baiting, but one that a beginner might use with some success, is to put out food for carrion-eaters. Motorists are familiar with the sight of magpies and crows feeding off the carcass of a hedgehog or rabbit at the roadside. For the cameraman who is not too squeamish about what he puts into the car boot, an hour's drive in the country fairly early in the morning can provide plenty of similar bait, which he can use to tempt magpies, crows and even buzzards to his pre-arranged filming location.

If filming can only be carried out on one day at the weekend, it is of considerable help if the chosen spot can be regularly baited several days prior to this by another member of the family or by a helper. When a regular supply of food is put out it is surprising how quickly the birds respond to it, and this preparation can greatly increase the chances of filming success. Carrion bait should be secured to the ground by means of a peg and fine nylon twine of the type that cannot be seen by the camera. If this is not done and there is an argument between two contenders for the prize, the bait may well be carried off.

One word of warning: bait ought never to be put down in areas where guns are used.

COURTSHIP AND AGGRESSION

Courtship behaviour may often be filmed from a hide set up to obtain nesting sequences, particularly if the work is being carried out in the middle of a colony. Some species such as the black grouse, which are polygamous, have special display grounds, and for these the usual hide construction routine should be employed. In some areas, although display may go on throughout the day, the main activity of the cock birds usually occurs very early in the morning, sometimes even before sunrise, so the hide may have to be entered while it is still dark. On still mornings sounds carry a long way, and special care should be taken when moving about inside the hide. The mechanical whirring of the camera should be muffled by winding a couple of old pullovers or some other thick material around it.

The easiest way of filming aggression is to provoke it. Aggressive behaviour can easily be induced in birds of certain species by placing a stuffed specimen of a male within the territory of its live counterpart. A male robin will very quickly peck to pieces such a specimen of its own kind. Stuffed foxes and owls set in suitable positions are rapidly mobbed by small birds whose reaction is so intense that a hide is scarcely necessary for filming. But the usefulness of staged experiments of this kind is limited, and they are mainly of scientific interest. Aggression against live intruders on a territory is another matter and is best caught on film by patience and opportunism.

FLIGHT

Flight is an important aspect of bird behaviour, yet it is very difficult to film well. With good camera operation, flight shots can provide a sequence of great beauty, but erratic camera work frequently leads to an irritating and ugly mess on the screen. Usually the trouble arises from the cameraman's over-confidence in his ability to hand-hold the camera.

It is much easier to hold a camera following a moving object than to keep it on a static framing. A hand-held camera may be used to film a kestrel in level flight without trouble; but a telephoto shot of a kestrel hovering is most unsatisfactory without a tripod, because in order to record faithfully the fixed position of the kestrel in space it is necessary for the bird to appear in a rigidly fixed position with respect to the picture frame.

Generally speaking, it is unwise to try to film bird flight without a tripod if the lens in use is longer than 100mm on a 16mm camera, or 50mm on an 8mm camera. Even then, success with such lenses depends very much on the skill of the cameraman, and some sort of additional aid such as a pistol grip may be found helpful.

As soon as very long-focus lenses go onto the camera, the operator begins to experience new problems. One of these is locating the bird in the viewfinder. It is easy enough to spot a bird with the naked eye, but finding it through a reflex camera, using a lens with an angle of acceptance of just a few degrees, is quite another matter.

The solution lies in fitting the end of the lens with a sort of gun-sight. This may be a permanent fixture made of wire, or a temporary job knocked up in a few minutes from a small piece of cardboard and a piece of camera tape. The sight is then set in the correct position. First, the camera is lined up on a small object some two hundred yards away. The object is centred in the reflex viewfinder, and the camera is fixed in this position by tightening up the screws on the tripod head. Secondly, the gun-sight is adjusted on the side of the lens so that with one eye looking through the viewfinder, the other eye sees the point of the sight just over the object. Once the required position for the sight has been found, it is securely fixed and the camera is then ready for quick action.

As soon as a bird is sighted, the cameraman, while continuing to look at it, should put one eye to the viewfinder in the normal filming attitude. Then, with the aid of the eye not looking through the viewfinder, the camera is moved until the point of the sight covers the bird. The bird should now also be visible at the centre of frame in the reflex viewfinder. Even if the alignment is not quite correct the bird will almost certainly be somewhere in frame, and an immediate adjustment can be made for correct composition. By this method it is possible to use even a 600mm lens to film a bird in flight within a few seconds of actually seeing it, provided a fluid tripod head is also being used.

CAMERA OPERATION IN FLIGHT SHOTS

If the camera is following a bird in flight, the picture composition should be such that rather more room is given in front of the bird than behind it. Not only is the resultant picture more pleasing aesthetically, but it allows a margin of error if the camera panning is not in complete sympathy with the flight path of the bird (Fig 9).

At the time of filming, it is not usually known exactly how such flight shots are going to be edited into the rest of the film. For example, one particular flight shot might be used after a close-up of a take-off; or if the bird is a predator this same shot could be used as a meaningful cut-in denoting a first sign of danger to some other animal; or it could be shown between two reaction shots of a man watching through binoculars. It is desirable, therefore, to film the shot in such a way that it can be used for a variety of purposes: this means that the bird should be filmed entering frame at the beginning and leaving frame at the end of the shot. As soon as the bird has been found in the viewfinder and is being followed, the camera should be quickly panned on ahead until the frame is empty and at the same time the motor should be switched on. The panning action is then stopped and the bird flies into frame, whereupon the camera again starts following it for the length of the required shot. Once more the panning action is slowed down and stopped, and the bird flies on out of frame. Then, and only then, should the motor be stopped.

When editing the film, this shot would be valuable not only as a means of bringing a sequence to a close but also for providing continuity; the same bird could be picked up again in

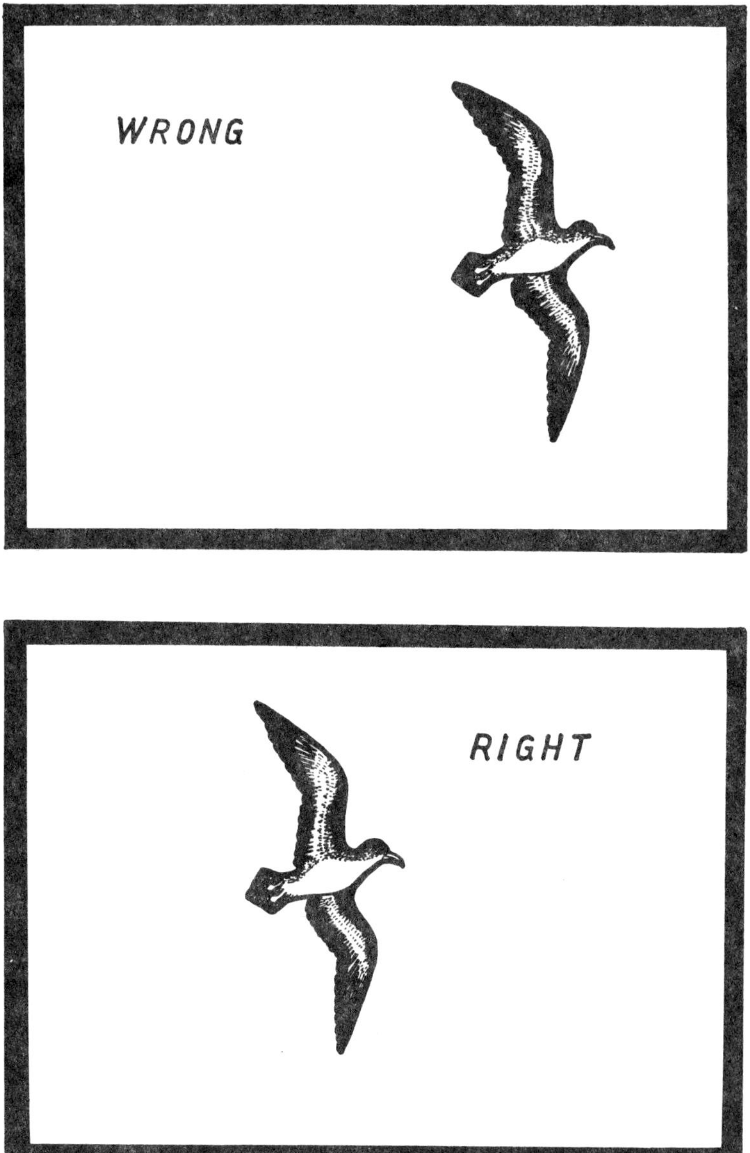

Fig 9 Composition of a flight shot

another scene, perhaps at some other location a considerable distance away.

With a smooth-running tripod head, there should be no great problems in filming birds moving approximately at right angles to the direction of the camera. But when birds fly towards, or diagonally towards camera, focus has to be adjusted continuously. With one eye on the viewfinder and one hand on the tripod handle, the other hand has to 'feel' focus as the bird approaches. Although this can be done with practice, a little preparation can save many shots from being spoiled. With a few rehearsal runs the cameraman can discover in which direction his hand has to turn to bring the focus forward. Then, without actually running the camera, he should practise following several birds in flight until by instinct he knows which way his hand must turn to hold focus.

If a clockwork camera is used to film a shot of long duration, the cameraman has to try to time it mentally, so that he completes his shot before the motor runs out. This again is an operation in which performance improves with practice.

It used to be the vogue some years ago for wildlife cameramen to film practically all bird flight in slow-motion. It seems to me pointless, however, to film indiscriminately in slow-motion unless an ultra-high-speed camera is available for detailed analysis of wing movements. Used with discretion, slow-motion sequences can of course be very beautiful. The best subjects are the large birds which flap rather than soar: swans, geese, ducks and, to a lesser extent, herons, egrets and flamingoes. To achieve the best results the birds should be filmed against a clear sky in good light. The light is most important when working at speeds of up to 64fps, because of the fast shutter speed and the required increase in exposure. Take-offs and landings make particularly good slow-motion shots, for the birds' wings are seen to go through some incredible movements. Here again, it is best to film larger birds, since the flap rate of anything smaller than a pigeon is so fast that normal cameras have insufficient speed to give worthwhile slow-motion.

If the camera is normally run at 24fps, then level-flight shots in slow-motion can be made at 48fps or 64fps. All take-offs and landings are best filmed at 64fps, if the light allows. If the camera is normally run at 16 or 18fps, then slow-motion speeds of 32, 48 or 64fps may be used.

Running the camera at 32fps when the normal is 24fps, or at 24fps when the normal is 16 or 18fps, does not provide sufficient difference to give much of a slow-motion effect, but it does have other uses. If normal flight scenes are being shot under adverse conditions, this slight difference in camera speed can help disguise uneven camera operation. It is even more effective in filming very small birds in close-up. Fast and erratic flight movements are slowed down just enough to make the pictures more acceptable on the screen, but not so much as to make the birds appear to be moving at an abnormally slower speed.

FILMING BIRDS FROM MOTOR VEHICLES

In many countries birds have already begun to accept the movement and noise of motor traffic with seeming indifference, even at close quarters. Motorists cannot fail to notice this. Even on motorways, magpies, crows and rooks seem to be able to gauge a vehicle's speed and usually fly up in front of it only just in time to avoid being run over, and kestrels hover unconcernedly above the grass verges as traffic screams past. A wide variety of birds can be observed from a car parked by the roadside in moorland, heath or forest, or by a river or estuary. Most birds accept a parked car if the doors are not opened and this provides fine opportunities for photography.

Although the birds may be close, they are not likely to be so close that the tripod can be dispensed with. This is a major problem, for unless the car is a large one it is difficult to get a tripod in position inside. If the front passenger seat is removable, however, a tripod with unexpanded legs can sometimes be set up so that the camera looks out of the passenger window, which should be wound down cautiously beforehand. Alternatively, a special attachment to take the tripod head may be clamped onto the passenger door when the window is wound down. The advantage of having the camera fixed in the front of the car is that it can be operated by one person, the driver.

Without doubt the best vehicle to film birds from is a minibus or something similar, with a sliding side door. A special hide front can be fixed up when the door is in the open position, and there is then plenty of room inside to operate comfortably.

Needless to say, the rules of the road are not obligingly suspended for photographers. Where stopping is permissible, care should be taken not to cause an obstruction or to block any other driver's view of oncoming traffic. But there are still many places in the world where one can pull well off the main roads, and numerous country tracks on which, with permission, it is possible to drive and park without inconvenience to anyone.

It is also well worth looking out for parks and sanctuaries where there are private roads or tracks for access. In 1969 I made a film in the United States about some of the Wildlife Refuges used by migrating wildfowl. In nearly all these refuges it was possible to drive within good filming range of normally jumpy ducks and geese. The major part of the film was shot by Ronald Eastman, operating a telephoto lens from the back of a large estate car. The only difficulty we experienced was that as the best camera position was just inside the tail door, all the driving at the refuges had to be in reverse!

6

Mammals Big and Small

THOSE who are fortunate enough to visit the great National Wildlife Parks of East Africa may be excused if they come away with the idea that filming wild mammals is easy. There, many of the animals take little or no notice of cars, and as camera subjects they pose no greater problems than birds – indeed, as most of them are considerably larger they are therefore easier to film in close-up.

Unfortunately this state of affairs is not general throughout the world, and usually anyone setting out to film wild mammals, whether in an American forest or an English wood, soon finds himself embarked on a battle of wits that makes great demands on his stamina, patience and photographic ingenuity.

The first fact to be faced up to – and it dominates all filming techniques in this field – is that these animals have an acute sense of smell. With birds scent is not a problem, and provided the cameraman keeps out of *sight* and reasonably quiet he has a good chance of success. With mammals a conventional hide is rarely used, since keeping out of sight is of secondary importance. Usually, on-the-spot camouflage has to do, for everything must be geared to mobility and the need to make a silent approach from downwind. Once in a filming position, the cameraman must work noiselessly. For this reason practically all wild-mammal filming in Britain has to be done with the camera in a blimp (see page 30), unless very long-focus lenses can be used under favourable wind conditions. But so many mammals have to be filmed in marginal light conditions that the limitations imposed by the working aperture of the lens make very long lenses impracticable and a blimp essential.

PREPARATIONS FOR FILMING

Although a conventional hide is not often used, preparations for filming the larger British or North American mammals take much longer than those necessary for the filming of birds. The reason is that the habits of these mammals vary a great deal from county to county, even from one area to another within a county. Roe deer may be much tamer in one county than another; badgers in one area may emerge from their setts or burrows a good half-hour later than those at setts only ten miles away. All such details the cameraman must find out by observation before he can expose a foot of film. Eric Ashby, Britain's leading cine photographer of wild mammals, maintains that for every day he goes out with his camera there are at least three or four days spent on reconnaissance. Then for every six days spent with the camera, five may provide no film at all: perhaps the light is not good enough, or the wind is in the wrong direction for filming at the desired earth or sett, or disturbance by foresters or hikers has made the animals more than usually wary.

When a suitable film location has been found – it may be an earth or a sett or a rutting ground – the first thing to do is to see if there is a convenient camera position. For larger mammals the filming distance to aim for at the start is around twenty yards, though this may have to be increased for wild deer. It may even be reduced to twenty feet when filming fox or badger cubs without the presence of their parents.

In choosing a camera position, the following should be taken into account:

1 direction of prevailing wind: ideally, the wind should blow from subject to camera, never from camera to subject (windless days are best left alone)
2 field of view: if possible, all entrances to setts and earths should be visible
3 conspicuousness of camera and cameraman: a silhouette on the skyline should be avoided at all costs; ideally, there should be a background of trees and bushes, but a fairly steep bracken-covered slope will do
4 ease of approach: the desired camera position must be taken up without fuss and noise, and without the cameraman's scent blowing across the area under observation at any time

Some preparatory work may be involved in satisfying conditions 2 and 4. A few twigs may block the view of one of the entrances to the earth or sett and may have to be removed with a penknife; it is recommended that this be done weeks in advance, and ideally in winter. When filming eventually takes place the cameraman will have both hands fully occupied in carrying camera, blimp and tripod, so it will probably not be possible to push brambles and branches to one side on the way to the filming position. Any such thorny obstacles *on the way* should be tied back or trimmed, and dry twigs underfoot removed, so that the approach is unhindered and noiseless. But none of these preparations should be attempted near earth or sett where the subject may pick up the scent.

Even with all these preparations, success is by no means assured. It could happen that on the first day appointed for filming the wind will completely change direction and be blowing from the camera position *towards* the place where the subject is expected to appear. Should this be the case, it is better to cut one's losses and spend the time doing something else. Even if the wind is right, no animal may be seen, perhaps because of some previous disturbance. Such are the trials of wild-mammal photography.

DEER

For much of the year deer are difficult to locate, so the spare-time cameraman would be wise to seek the advice of local farmers, gamekeepers and foresters. Even they may have no definite information; but someone might have heard that a small herd of fallow deer was in such-and-such a place two days ago, or that two roe deer are often seen at the edge of a certain wood just after dawn. From here on, the cameraman must follow his rules, be patient in waiting or stalking, and hope for luck.

Some seasons and places afford better opportunities than others for finding deer. In Scotland, during the harder months of the year, red deer can sometimes be filmed on lower ground by the edges of lochs in the first hour or two of daylight. When there is a good depth of snow, fallow and roe deer can be located by following their tracks. Fallow deer can also be located in early spring when they are feeding well on young and succulent food; in early summer they tend to lie up in cover for much of the day, away from the flies.

For most of the year film shots of wild deer will never provide much in the way of action, just a few pleasant grazing scenes and a sense of achievement in having actually got them in the camera. The big opportunity for the film-maker comes with the rut. With roe deer this takes place in early summer. In some areas the rutting activities are concentrated in places known as 'rings'. These are circular tracks, usually around a small tree or other herbage which is taller than the surrounding vegetation. If these can be located whilst they are still in use by the deer, it should be possible to film a fascinating sequence. To my knowledge, however, no cameraman has yet succeeded in filming the rutting of roe deer really satisfactorily; so for someone here is a golden opportunity to score a 'first'.

Autumn sequences of the rut of fallow and red deer have been filmed on many occasions, with particularly striking results. Here, the roaring of the bucks and stags gives some guide to the actual rutting area, which will be used for several weeks providing there is no undue disturbance. Eric Ashby has filmed the fallow deer of the New Forest at their rut for many years. He usually aims to get to his camera position about forty minutes before starting to film at dawn, or as soon as there is enough light available for an exposure. On these occasions it is foolish to be too early, because a sudden change of wind direction can give the cameraman's presence away whilst he is still waiting for the light.

By repeated visits to a rutting area it is possible to collect a great variety of shots of different behaviour: the buck calling, marking territory, rounding up the does, sparring with and chasing off challenging bucks, and actual mating. In this way a meaningful film sequence, or even a short film, can gradually be built up.

FOXES

Foxes are fairly common, so there is always the chance that one might pass by while the cameraman is waiting for something else to happen. The chances are quite high in early January, when the foxes are looking for mates; but the most rewarding time to film them is from March onwards, when cubs may be seen at the earth.

Success in obtaining good close-ups of the cubs depends to a large extent on whether the vixen is with them or not. If she is, then a good deal of caution must be exercised, for she will be on the alert all the time. If she is not at the earth and the cubs are quite young, a very slow and cautious approach, edging forward a foot or two at a time, may lead to a rewarding shot. There must be no sudden movement; every action should be carried out as if in slow-motion; and if no sound is made and the background is such that the cameraman's outline does not appear against the sky, it may be possible to get within ten yards. If the earth is in an exposed position on a moor, this sort of approach may not be feasible. One naturalist solved the problem quite neatly by camouflaging himself and his camera behind a mask and sheepskin, thus presenting the familiar front view of one of the local moorland sheep.

If the vixen is not with the cubs when they appear above ground, it is usually extremely difficult to get any pictures at all of her returning to them with food. This is probably because a returning vixen often 'walks around' the earth and in so doing passes behind the cameraman and gets his scent. He should therefore keep an eye open for an approach from any direction.

BADGERS

It is often said that badger-watching is best done from a low branch of a tree, but to the cameraman the advantages of being up a tree are minimal unless the added height gives very much better coverage over undulating ground. The complications of filming from a branch are considerable: not least among them the building of a stable platform for the tripod, or the fixing of a bracket to the trunk for mounting the tripod head and camera. When filming from ground level the only additional point to watch is that the camera position should not be too close to any of the badger paths radiating from the sett.

Fifteen years ago it was thought that the only practical way to film wild badgers was to condition them to artificial lighting. Dr Ernest Neal and Professor Humphrey Hewer were pioneers in this (British television viewers may remember

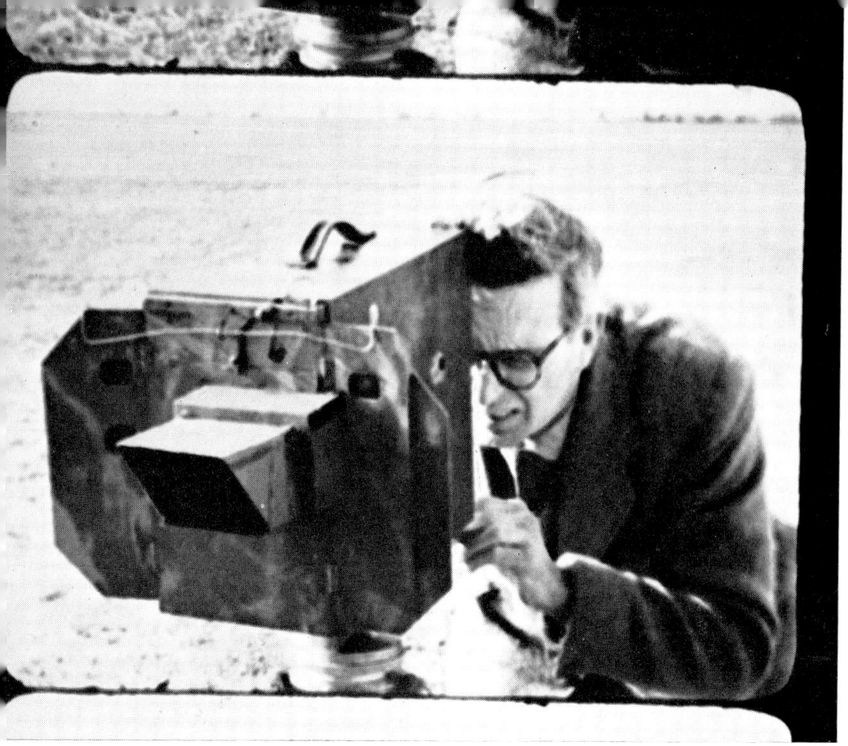

Page 87 Two scenes from *Look – A Hare's Life*: (*above*) the stalker, Eric Ashby, using a home-made blimp, but in an exposed mid-field position, creeps slowly forward. Note the side flaps to hide the cameraman's face; (*below*) the stalked: a big close-up of a wild hare taken in an open field by Eric Ashby a few yards away.

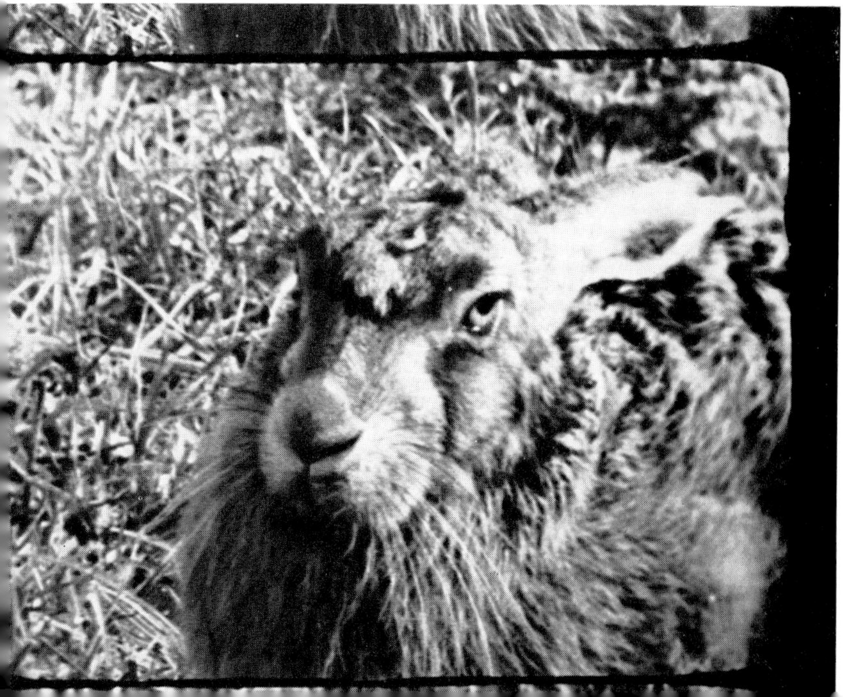

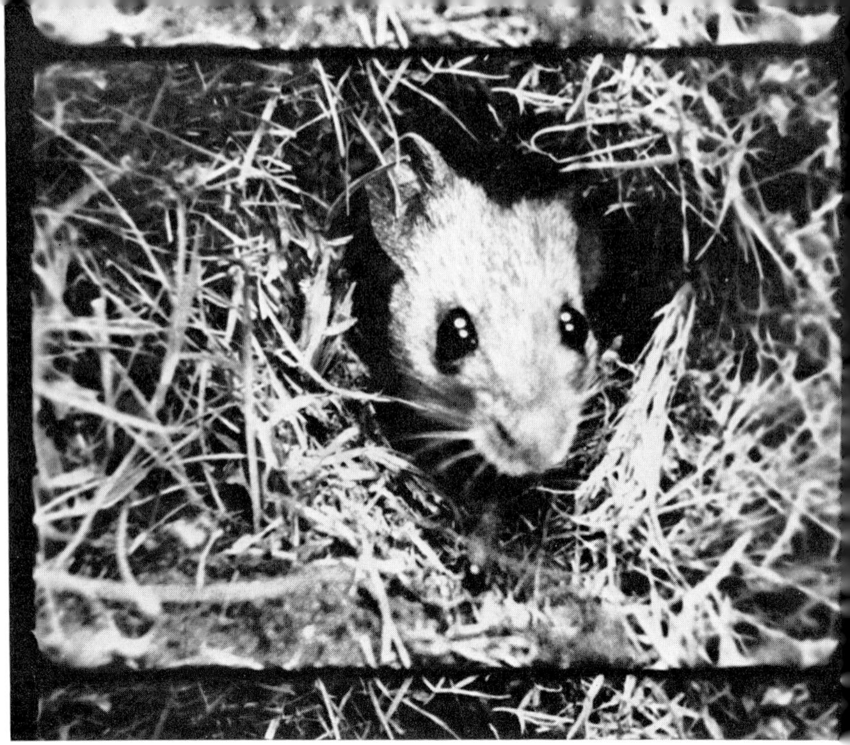

Page 88 Two scenes from *Look – Town Mouse and Country Mouse* filmed by Leslie Jackman and Ronald Peggs: (*above*) long-tailed field mouse appears above ground – filmed in compartment A of set similar to that shown in Fig 10; (*below*) long-tailed field mouse with store of nuts underground – filmed in compartment B of a set similar to that shown in Fig. 10.

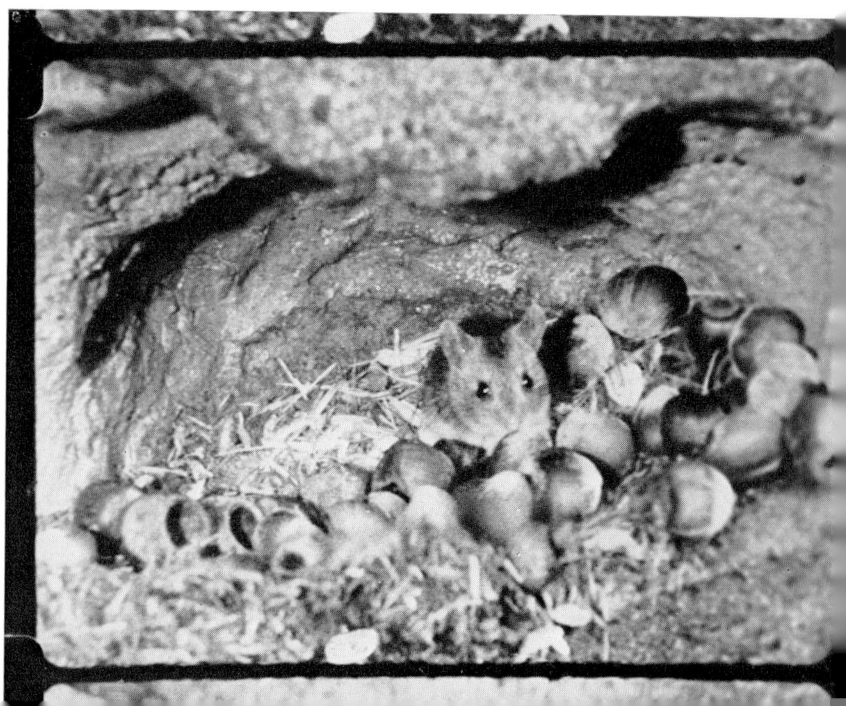

their remarkable film, which was shown in an early natural history programme in 1954). A few years later I began to condition badgers in my father's garden in Devon, at a sett conveniently situated about twenty-five yards from the house. I began with a 25W lamp which gave the effect of a good moonlit night, and over a period of many weeks gradually increased the brightness, just as Neal and Hewer had done. I had hopes of improving on existing badger film: the sett was in a good position, the animals were used to human activity close by, and a long period of conditioning was possible. But by the time the illumination was nearly bright enough for filming, Eric Ashby had been discovered. His film of badgers in natural light was so outstanding that it made all efforts to film under artificial light quite pointless.

Eric Ashby's success with badgers has been achieved by a combination of skill and patience, and by the discovery that badgers at some remote setts in the New Forest emerge in comparatively good light at certain times of the year. Even at these particular setts things are not easy. To all the usual difficulties of wind direction and need for avoidance of all noise and disturbance, is added the light factor. Most setts are situated under trees or bushes, and an evening with good light is essential if any advantage is to be taken of the very short time between the emergence of the badgers and the setting of the sun. But, with perseverance, Ashby has shown that it is possible to film badgers in good colour as well as in black and white.

If there is no alternative to working at a sett where the badgers emerge late, or if artificial lights are being used, it is sometimes possible to coax out the badgers by regular baiting. To be of much use, this must be done with a mixture of kitchen scraps night after night, so that the badgers' natural fear of human scent is partially overcome by their eagerness for the free meals which they gradually learn to expect near their sett entrance.

Although I myself have only succeeded in getting one or two cubs to take bait somewhat nervously and reluctantly, I have seen the Leicestershire naturalist John Whall use this method to coax out an entire family in front of a full sound-film crew using lights. This is remarkable, but there are drawbacks to this sort of badger filming. The animals may get used to lights and even human scent, but they are all the time *aware* of these things and this, coupled with their feeding on unnatural food, results in behaviour that is also to some degree unnatural, and therefore of limited value to the serious wildlife film-maker.

RABBITS AND HARES

By sticking to the rules and sitting comfortably near a rabbit warren, no cameraman should have difficulty in getting film shots of rabbits. Indeed, like birds, they too can often be photographed from cars.

Hares are quite another matter. They frequent large open fields where there is little or no cover, and the best plan is to stalk them. The time to get good action is from the end of February onwards when the hares start indulging in the mad capers associated with their territorial rights and pairing.

Filming hares means an early start; the cameraman should be on the scene at dawn, ready to run the camera as soon as light permits. When the hares have been located, they should be approached very slowly in a straight line, from a down-wind direction. The camera in its blimp should already be fixed to the tripod, and carried forward a few steps at a time. Movements such as picking up and putting down the camera should be slow, and the cameraman would be well advised to keep his face down behind the camera blimp as far as possible. Eric Ashby, who has taken some of the best studies of wild hares, had a flap fixed on both sides of the blimp to help conceal the whiteness of his face.

A very slow straight-line approach can take a cameraman within easy filming range, but sometimes a second factor plays a part: the hares' own inquisitiveness. Provided the movements of this new 'scarecrow' are imperceptible to the hares, they may even approach it to investigate. This curiosity can be exploited in another way, by deliberately placing a new object in the hares' field, some twenty yards from a hedgerow, and filming from the cover of the hedge. The object could be just a large log of wood, but it would probably attract the hares, and if only a close-up or two is required, this may be the best method to use.

THE PHOTOGENIC WATER VOLE

Of all the British mammals, the water vole provides one of the best possibilities for the beginner in cine photography. A sunny bank in which there are several water-vole holes should be found and the camera set up on the opposite bank. Having settled himself into a comfortable position, with a good background of bushes or reeds, the cameraman just sits and waits. With patience, good shots of a most photogenic animal can be obtained even without the use of a blimp. Yet the water vole remains ignored by the majority of wildlife cameramen.

The habits of otters, on the other hand, are such that any filming other than that of the opportunist type is almost impossible in Britain – with the possible exception of part of Scotland. Even more difficult are the wild cat, pine marten and polecat, which are so rare that they have seldom been filmed.

OTHER SMALL MAMMALS

For most of us the other mammals available are small and, except for hedgehogs and squirrels, need to be filmed under controlled conditions.

The acrobatic jumps of squirrels are best filmed in the winter months, when the leafless trees enable good length shots to be taken; but unless these are filmed on a sunny day the results can be disappointing, and even on colour film the images will be little more than silhouettes. To get good close-ups the squirrels can be baited down a tree with acorns and other nuts, though autumn is a good time to film them gathering food for themselves.

Bait can also be used to get shots of field mice or voles, but anything approaching full cine studies of these creatures can only be made by setting up a family of them in captivity. This can be a time-consuming operation and involves the construction of a 'set' in a shed or spare room. Therefore, it should not be undertaken without careful consideration of what is entailed.

Before filming small mammals under controlled conditions it is necessary to:

1 design and build a suitable set
2 catch the required animals
3 condition them to their new home and to artificial lights

Fig 10 shows a set similar to one designed and built by Leslie Jackman and Ronald Peggs for filming long-tailed field mice for a British television programme. It could also be used for housing other species that burrow.

Various changes may be made to the habitat in the upper, above-ground, compartment A, whilst the animals are in residence in compartment B. For example, turf could be used to simulate a section of meadow, or hazel twigs bearing ripe nuts could be arranged to simulate part of a hedgerow. The important thing is that the floor of compartment A, which lies directly over the subterranean compartment B, should be hard enough to prevent the mice or voles from burrowing where it is not intended. The same applies to compartment B itself, which is shaped out of concrete to provide runs and

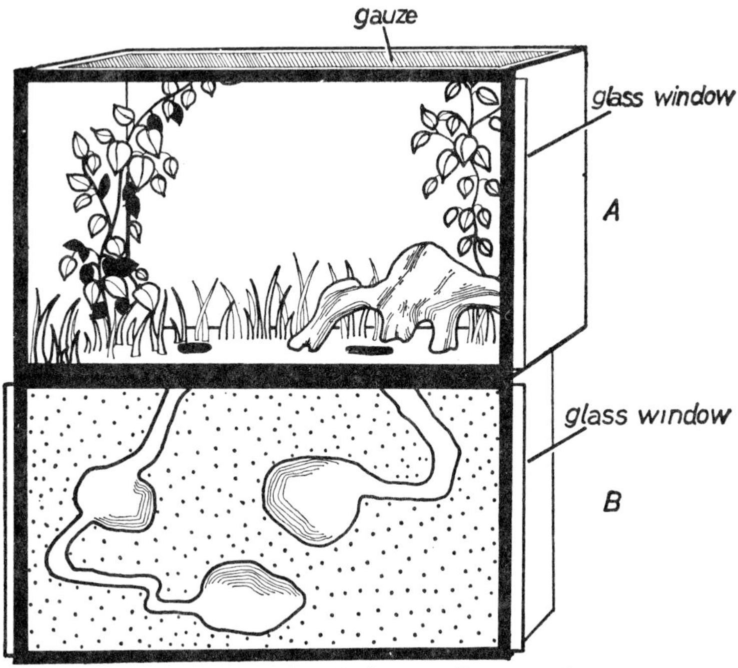

Fig 10 Set for filming small mammals

nesting chambers. Compartment B is very narrow, so that all the underground activities of the animals can be observed through the front glass window. Plain concrete looks most unnatural, but this can be remedied by throwing soil at it before it finally sets (this is done when the concrete has been shaped in its box in a horizontal position). At the same time, bits of tree-root fibre and similar items can be pressed into the side of the burrows to aid the necessary deception.

The main problem with compartment B is that the inside of the glass is likely to get dirty very quickly as a result of the activities of the animals near it. The only solution is for the glass panel to be mounted in such a way that it can be slid out for cleaning. An identical sheet of glass must be slid in from the other end as the first is removed, to prevent the animals from escaping. An escape-proof cover, made of fine metal gauze to provide ventilation, should also be fitted to the top of compartment A.

Most small mammals are mainly nocturnal in their habits, so lights have to be introduced very gradually. As with badgers, a start should be made with a very low-power lamp left on near the enclosure all night, and the illumination increased slowly every few days. By the time the illumination gives a good working light, the animals may tolerate a sudden increased brightness during filming without concern. This is important. If full lighting were used all the time, the rise in temperature in the cage would undoubtedly cause suffering.

Jackman and Peggs found that the time taken between the setting up of their colony of field mice and the commencement of filming was about twelve weeks. Even then, although the mice became used to lights, they were still afraid of humans and it was found that filming had to be conducted from behind a screen.

7

Aquariums

AQUARIUMS can be used for complete life-history cine studies, but often their most valuable use lies in providing a welcome glimpse of an underwater world in a more general ecological film. If this is to be convincing, however, a great deal of attention must be paid to designing the layout of the aquarium, or 'dressing the set'. Most small forms of marine and freshwater life can only be filmed in a tank, and the more authentic the composition of this micro-habitat, the more natural will be the behaviour of its inhabitants and the more readily will the audience accept the film without questioning how it was achieved.

A SUITABLE TANK

Aquarists will already have most of the equipment necessary to start filming, but for the cameraman who has never stocked a tank the additional cost is not great. If freshwater, tropical and marine species are likely to be filmed at one time or another, then it is best to acquire a tank that will do for all three. Good carpenters may prefer to build their own, using wood for the base, back and two sides, and a single sheet of glass for the front. Otherwise, an angle-iron rectangular tank may be bought at most pet shops. It is as well to have the polythene-dipped variety, as iron rusts very quickly in contact with sea-water. Alternatively, stainless-steel frame tanks may be used.

Tank-size depends on the size of the subject to be filmed, but for most creatures up to three or four inches the best general-purpose tank measures 24 × 12 × 10in. This may appear slightly limiting at first, but the scene inside the tank can be varied at will by changing the position of the stones and plants with which the set is dressed. The effect of this can be heightened if the background is changed too.

For a wooden tank the background is painted on the back wall, using dark greens and browns to simulate underwater plant growth, and grey patterns to simulate rocks in the case of marine pools. If an angle-iron aquarium is used, it is more convenient to paint backgrounds on cards that can then be clamped vertically just behind the outside of the rear wall. These do not necessarily have to be works of art, since they will be mainly out of focus anyway, but they do nevertheless help to give the impression of depth. If transparencies of underwater scenes are available, an even more sophisticated and authentic-looking background can be achieved by back-projecting these onto a translucent screen immediately behind the aquarium.

WATER AND PLANTS

The necessity for really clean water cannot be overstated. Aquarium water may appear to be clear to the naked eye, but when photographed under bright lights all sorts of dirt and decaying food may show up. If such matter is present, it will particularly affect shots taken with lenses of a narrow angle of acceptance; close-ups will appear to be not quite in focus, sometimes rather as though they are being viewed through a white veil.

This sort of thing can be prevented to a great extent by carefully washing any sand that is put in the bottom of the tank. This must be done over and over again, until the water tipped away from the last wash is absolutely clear. The same applies to stones and also to plants.

In freshwater aquariums, plants will probably play an important part in each set. It is generally advisable to plant out the aquarium about a week or ten days before the livestock is introduced, to allow the plants to settle. Initially, these will have to be anchored into the sand with a small stone attached to the roots, or alternatively a small piece of lead can be lightly coiled around the stem near the roots.

When planting out a set in an aquarium, it is easy to get carried away in one's efforts to make the whole thing look authentic. The desired effect can usually be achieved quite simply, by the use of a suitable background and no more than a few plants and stones. If too many are used, there will be far too much cover and the animal subjects will hide away out of camera range.

Planting has to be done with the tank at least half full of water, which in the case of freshwater aquariums may nearly always be drawn from the tap. If this water supply is very heavily chlorinated, however, clear spring or stream water should be used instead. For marine aquariums sea-water should be collected from a large rock-pool, or direct from the sea, when the weather is calm and the water clear. If regular supplies of fresh sea-water are not available, sea-salt for making up sea-water can be bought at pet shops.

UPKEEP AND STOCK

It is very simple to maintain a freshwater aquarium that is not overcrowded and has a few plants; an adequate food supply for its occupants is all that is required. Marine aquariums need a little more attention: two essential items for keeping the inhabitants healthy and the water clean are an aerator motor and a sub-sand filter. The aerator, connected by tubing to a diffuser stone, keeps the water well oxygenated, and together with the sub-sand filter helps to keep it free from dirt. The filter is covered with sand, and acts in such a way that the water is drawn down into it, cleaned, and expelled again near the surface. Although most of the filter is out of sight, the tubing that leads to it is not, and must either be kept to one corner out of the picture frame when filming, or hidden by a suitable rock or plant. To avoid tell-tale currents and bubbles, both aerator and filter should be turned off during filming.

The filmscript determines the stock that goes into the aquarium, but careful thought has to be given to the order in which various species are introduced in relation to the available filming time. For example, it is no good stocking an aquarium with Dytiscus larvae and tadpoles, with the idea of returning a week or so later to film one catching the other. Long before that, there will have been a massacre and only Dytiscus will await the camera.

For predator-prey situations the two species are kept in different containers, and the predator is not fed for several days before filming. It may therefore be necessary to have several separate aquariums solely for the purpose of keeping specimens in, and for these an assortment of large jars and wide-necked confectionery bottles can be used.

LIGHTING AQUARIUMS

For most small aquariums, sufficient lighting is provided by two 500W photofloods. Since it is natural for almost all the light to come directly from above in underwater sequences, one lamp can be suspended above the surface of the water; but to bring out the colours on the sides of fish and other creatures one or more lamps will be required to the side of the camera position, and directed diagonally towards the aquarium.

This creates a problem of reflection. To correct it, the

camera should be set up for the widest angle shot, and it should then be possible (assuming that a rectangular tank is being used) to pan the camera a little to the left and the right before the corners of the aquarium come into view. The whole of this field can then be studied through the reflex viewfinder to see if any lamp reflections are visible. If there are reflections a lamp may have to be moved slightly, but a position can always be found where no reflected lights are seen from a given camera stand.

The second problem that lighting creates is that of increased water temperature. Without precautions, two 500W lamps close to a small tank could heat the water at an alarming rate, and in a short time the occupants would begin to suffer and even die. In freshwater tanks, a continuous supply of cold water direct from the tap (unless, of course, this is heavily chlorinated) keeps the temperature down. Alternatively, a pump can be used to circulate the water through tubes coiled in a bucket of ice or through some other cooling device. The pump system has to be used in marine tanks, where an unlimited supply of clean sea-water is not available.

The most sensible way to avoid a rising water temperature is to use photographic lights only when the camera is actually running. This means that the working light has to be just bright enough to enable the cameraman to see what is going on and to focus, but sufficiently distant not to have a marked heating effect on the water. If its colour temperature is not the same as the photographic lights, the working light should not be bright enough to give an exposure at the working aperture on the camera.

Photographic lights can be used more economically if the switch for them is within arm's reach of the camera position. Otherwise an assistant will be needed to control the lights while the cameraman concentrates solely on operating the camera.

SPECIAL FILMING TECHNIQUES

It is extremely useful to have an assistant when undertaking any type of controlled filming, be it in an aquarium or vivarium. When a new animal is added to the film set, quick action may result, and the cameraman needs to be in his camera position and fully on the alert. There is often some stage-managing to be done too, for some creatures have to be dissuaded from getting into positions not easily covered by the camera. The term 'ackler' seems to have been coined for an assistant doing this sort of work.

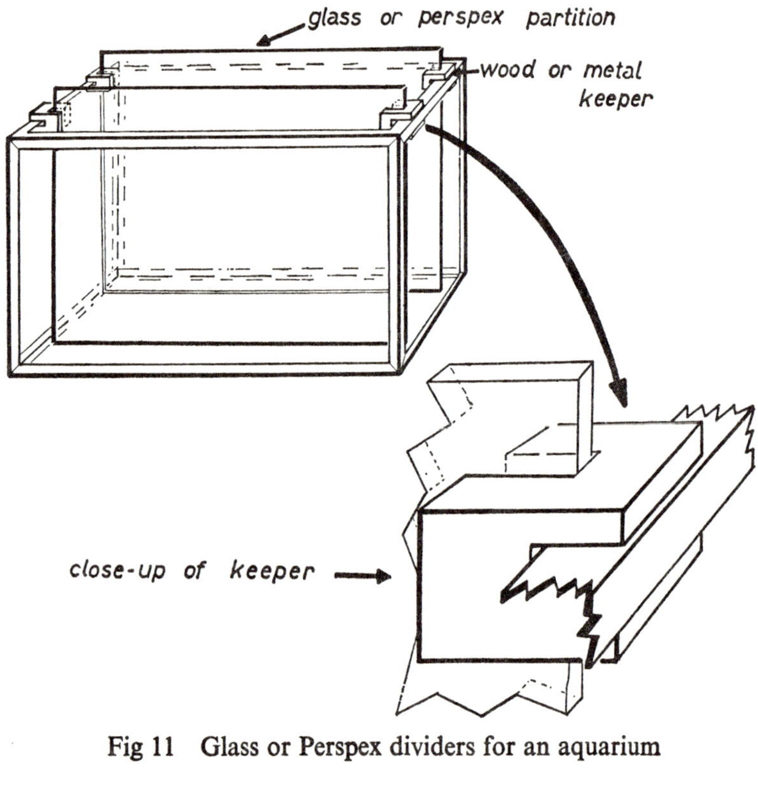

Fig 11 Glass or Perspex dividers for an aquarium

A pair of wooden tongs is a useful implement for shifting shellfish, crabs and other marine creatures around on the bottom of the tank; and to keep free-swimming fish in one part of the tank and in focus for an appreciable time, a divider can be used (see Fig 11). This should be made of glass or strong transparent plastic such as 'Perspex'. This divider is rectangular and a fraction smaller than the front glass window of the aquarium. It is held vertically in position in the water by wooden or metal keepers that fit along the two topside edges of the tank. If necessary, two or more sheets of glass can be inserted to keep specimens in a desired plane for the composition of certain establishing wide angles, and this method may also be found useful when close-ups are required. However, with small specimens, especially those measuring less than an inch, there is a better way of obtaining close-ups, and that is to use a very much smaller aquarium. Where a fair amount of aquarium filming is being carried out it is well worth preparing a whole range of tiny containers suitable for filming close-ups. These are cells, made either out of two pieces of glass with a wooden base and sides (Fig 12), or entirely of Perspex.

Perspex has good optical qualities but great care has to be taken when handling it as it scratches easily. Cells are easy to make in this material because the edges of the five pieces can be fused together quickly with choloroform. The resultant containers create fewer lighting problems than those with wooden sides. The dimensions can be tailored to suit requirements without causing discomfort to the animal being filmed: the smallest could be 1in wide × 1in high × $\frac{3}{8}$in deep; and a large one 4in × 3in × 1in. It is especially important to make the cells thin enough, from front to back, to restrict the movements of the subject and prevent it moving out of focus.

When a close-up is required, the creature is transferred to the cell and placed immediately in front of the aquarium that

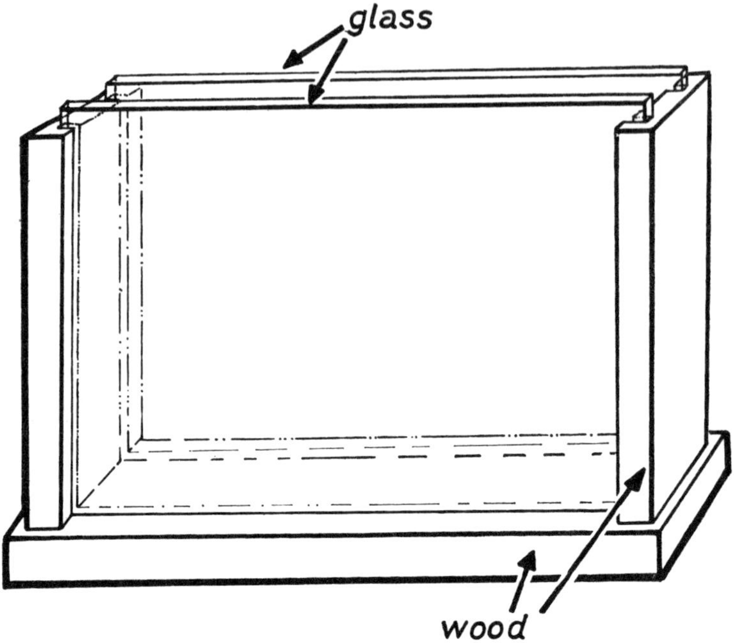

Fig 12 A miniature aquarium (actual size) for filming big close-ups

is being used for the main film sequences. This ensures that the background for the close-ups matches that of the wider shots of the same animal taken in the main aquarium, and that the two will intercut.

Before introducing the subject into the cell, it is advisable to line up and focus the camera on a dummy, and calculate an exposure. The live insect or fish should then be placed in the cell for the shortest possible time, since it may not only become short of oxygen but also get overheated under the lights in so small an amount of water. If much time is to be spent on a series of complicated close-ups, the heat from the lamps must be prevented from reaching the subject, and a means of doing this is described in the next chapter.

When the subject has to be kept in one of the medium-size

or larger cells for any length of time, the cell can be placed within the main aquarium so that the water surrounding it will help to dissipate the heat of the lights. The cell should rest on a suitable object so that its top is just above the level of the water, otherwise its occupant may escape. It should be noted that while the surrounding water may help to cool the subject, it will do little to prevent the infra-red rays of the lamps from falling onto it; water baths are an inefficient method of cooling light.

Apart from the widest angle scenes that the dimensions of the aquarium permit, and the close-ups that have already been discussed, there will of course be all sorts of intermediate shots possible. With a small aquarium there is usually not much scope for moving the camera position, so most of the variation of angle must come from changing the lens. This is not ideal, for in good film-making the position of the camera is never constant in respect of the subject. Other ways of achieving desirable changes of angle have to be sought. Often this can be done within the aquarium, simply by moving the animal subject and part of the set. This is particularly useful with slow-moving creatures that live on the bottom, for the key section of the set to be moved may be just a single stone.

Consider the following example: a series of shots is required of a hermit crab walking across to an empty shell, inspecting it, and transferring to it. Fig 13A shows the set-up for the first wide establishing shot which covers some of the journey of the crab in its original shell. As it nears the new shell a medium close shot is required, and this could be obtained by jumping in with a longer lens from the same camera position. But a better cut, and a better composed picture, could be obtained by first moving the position of the new shell and the rock immediately behind it to the position shown in Fig 13B; the hermit crab is then moved so that its angle of approach in relation to these is the same as it was in the first wide-angle

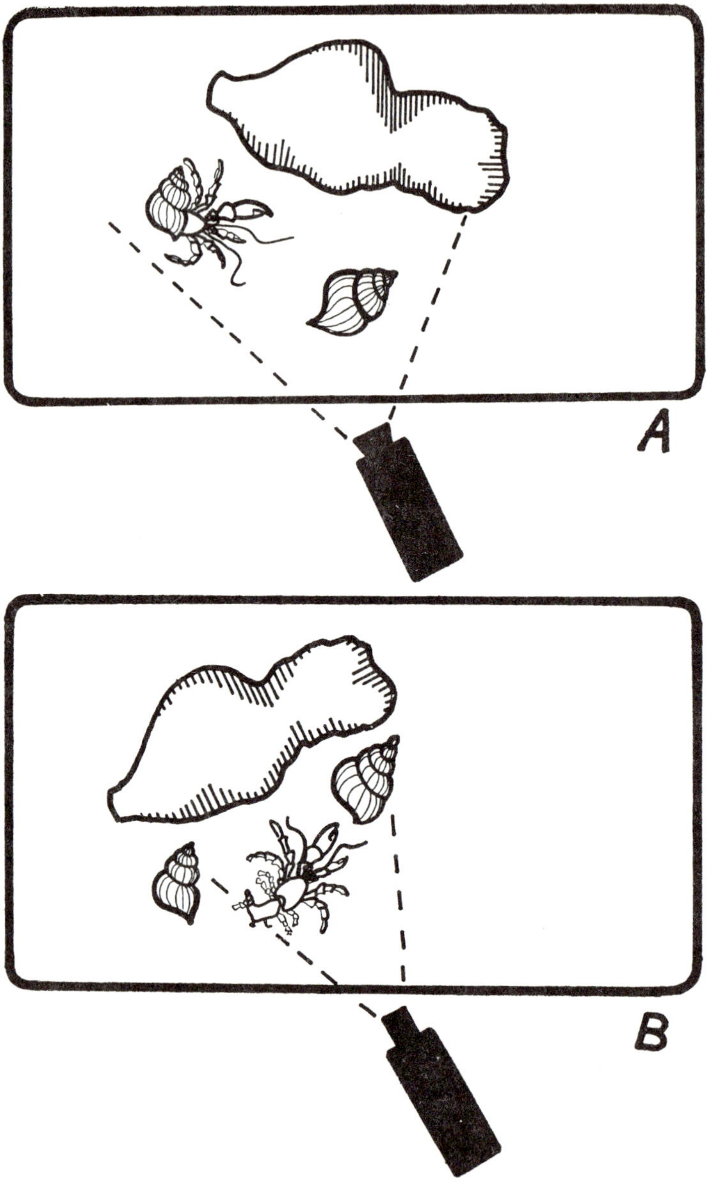

Fig 13 Changing the position of the set and subject in an aquarium instead of the camera and lights

shot. Although the camera and the lights remain virtually unchanged, there is an *effective* change of camera position. Methods of this kind can only be used with the lower forms of life, whose behaviour is fairly predictable.

CONTINUITY WITH OUTDOOR WORK

When aquarium sequences are to be integrated with above-water sequences to produce, for example, a film about pond life, every opportunity should be taken to film shots that will move the action naturally from below water to above, or vice versa. Each one of these will be of great help in making the aquarium scenes look authentic.

Insects that spend their lives part in and part out of water are particularly useful. For example, a dragonfly nymph is filmed climbing up a reed stem in an aquarium prior to undergoing its metamorphosis. It is allowed to pass out of frame near the surface. If this specimen or a similar one in the same stage is now taken to another above-water set, or even an actual pond with the same type of reeds, a valuable link shot can be obtained which not only continues the dragonfly story but helps to bind the aquarium material with the rest of the film.

Continuity with outdoor work can often be achieved very simply and effectively: a shot of a fisherman's hook and bait sinking in the aquarium, cut in immediately after a real fishing sequence, provides continuous action for the viewer to follow, leading his eye to underwater creatures before he has had time to realize that the shots must have been taken in an aquarium.

FILMING IN STREAMS

Although indoor aquariums can effectively simulate pond and even deep-river conditions, it is extremely difficult to set up anything in a tank that bears any resemblance to a shallow river or a stream. If small fish and other creatures are to be filmed in that setting, the only really convincing way to do it is to set up a tank in the stream itself (Fig 14). The two end 'walls' of the aquarium, a and b, are made of metal gauze, not glass or wood, and the running water flows straight through. This produces beautiful and completely authentic effects of bubbling water and weed movements under the pull of the current. (A larger grid of metal gauze can be placed upstream to hold back weeds and other floating debris.)

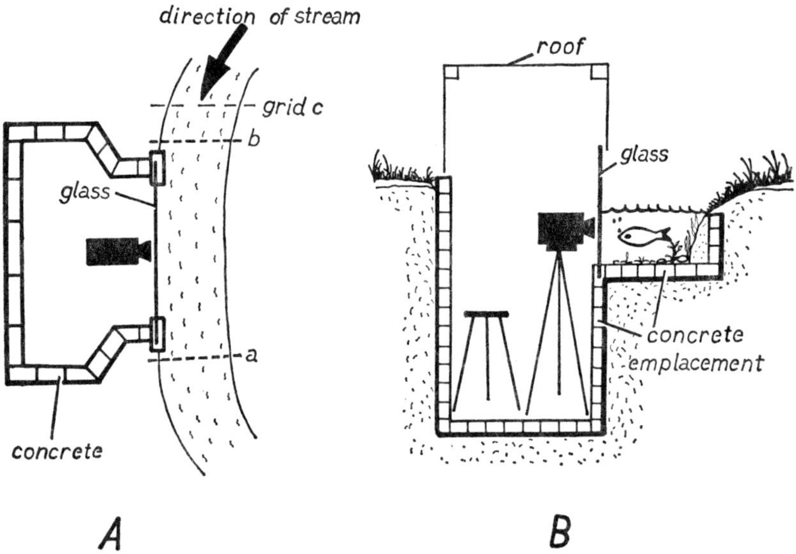

Fig 14 An out-of-doors aquarium in a stream

Such an operation can only be considered if one has a small stream or river on one's own land, or if the landowner concerned can be talked into agreeing to the excavations to make a suitable camera position at water-level. How this is done will depend on such things as the rise and fall of the ground close to the stream, soil factors and available building materials. In many cases it is best to build the camera emplacement, window, and adjacent walls a few feet away from, and parallel to, the stream (Fig 15). When preparations are completed, the stream is then diverted by digging out the ground separating it from the observation window. A fast-running stream soon settles into a natural-looking bed, but it can be helped by replacing the ground and stones from the old bed and replanting. A few square feet of polythene laid underneath the stones of the new stream bed will help prevent seepage into the camera emplacement.

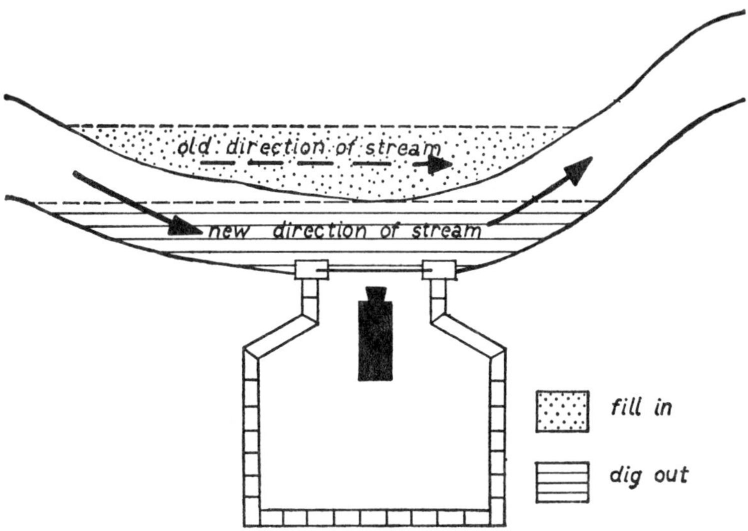

Fig 15 Building a stream aquarium

The above method of filming in a stream may be quite impracticable for many cameramen. However, provided the water is clear and the surface not too disturbed, they can sometimes get good shots of fish from above water. Spawning trout have been filmed in this way, and so has the courtship of newts.

When filming in this way, down through the surface of

water, reflections are quite a problem – not so much images of trees and bushes as patterns of light from the sky and sun. The light reflected is to some extent polarized, and this can largely be prevented from entering the lens by placing a polaroid filter in front of it. A reflex viewfinder is needed to make sure that it is correctly aligned; if the filter is then slowly rotated, a position can be found at which the reflections are at a minimum.

Another device for filming in shallow water has been developed by Peter Parks of Oxford Scientific Films. This is a periscope about three feet high, which is fitted directly onto a tripod head. The periscope has a watertight seal, which unfortunately makes it slightly awkward to operate, since it is buoyant and difficult to hold down in more than a few inches of water. However, it can be clamped down in a vertical position by securing it to a tripod leg. Some very effective sequences have been filmed with periscopes, but the device will undoubtedly have to be further developed and improved.

8

Insects and Small Things

I AM sometimes asked whether I think that there is any danger of the wildlife film-maker running out of new subject material. There is not much doubt about the answer. As yet, cameramen have made only small inroads into the hundreds of species of birds, mammals, reptiles and amphibians, and the thousands of insect species have scarcely been looked at – indeed new ones are being discovered at a faster rate than they can be filmed.

Insects have been comparatively neglected, which is a great pity because some of their life histories provide remarkable and at times almost unbelievable stories that make fascinating films. As some stages of an insect's life may be spent underground, or underwater, or inside a tree or even a leaf, the filming of them is a challenge, and demands not only a knowledge of entomology but a great deal of ingenuity. Because of the special problems in filming, and because most insects are so small, practically all insect photography has to be done under carefully controlled laboratory conditions. It is rare for a complete life history to be filmed in the field. The most that can normally be achieved are studies of the larger insects such as butterflies, moths, mantids, bees and wasps – and only incidents shot on an opportunist basis at that. These can usually be filmed without the use of highly sophisticated equipment, provided a few simple rules are observed.

INSECT FILMING IN THE FIELD

The scope of work in the field is inevitably determined by the lens system on the camera. Different makes of zoom differ in their range of focal lengths. One camera enables focus to be obtained on an object actually within the lens hood, though this introduces some shadow problems. In other cases supplementary lenses are available for close-up work, but a reflex camera must always be used, for both framing and focus are critical.

For insect close-ups it is essential that both camera and subject should be very steady. In the case of the camera the condition is satisfied by using a good tripod, but in the case of the subject the solution is not so easy. Insects on the ground or on trees or walls are not much of a problem, but those on leaves and plants are easily blown in and out of picture frame even by the lightest of winds. It is best to avoid this type of shooting on all but windless days, and there are few of these. It cannot be overemphasized that the slightest breath of wind can have a devastating effect on a big close-up: if the wind is blowing towards camera it takes the subject in and out of focus; if it is blowing across camera the subject appears to dance all over the place. It is very easy to dismiss the movement of a leaf as insignificant when it is moving only a few millimetres, but if the same movement is studied through the viewfinder it is obvious that it will be a movement of many inches, perhaps even a foot or two, when shown enlarged on a projection screen. The resulting picture may look so unsteady that it will be hardly viewable.

In the case of winged insects that fly from plant to plant there is little to be done other than to avoid windy days. If a number of butterflies are seen in a good filming position, it is better on the whole to keep back on a lens of longer focal length than try to get in close with a lens of short focal length. The two diagrams in Fig 16 indicate the reason why. In position 2 the camera can be swung round to cover most of the bush without too drastic a change in frame-size and focus. In position 1 the camera would be badly placed for close-ups of the butterflies in the two side positions.

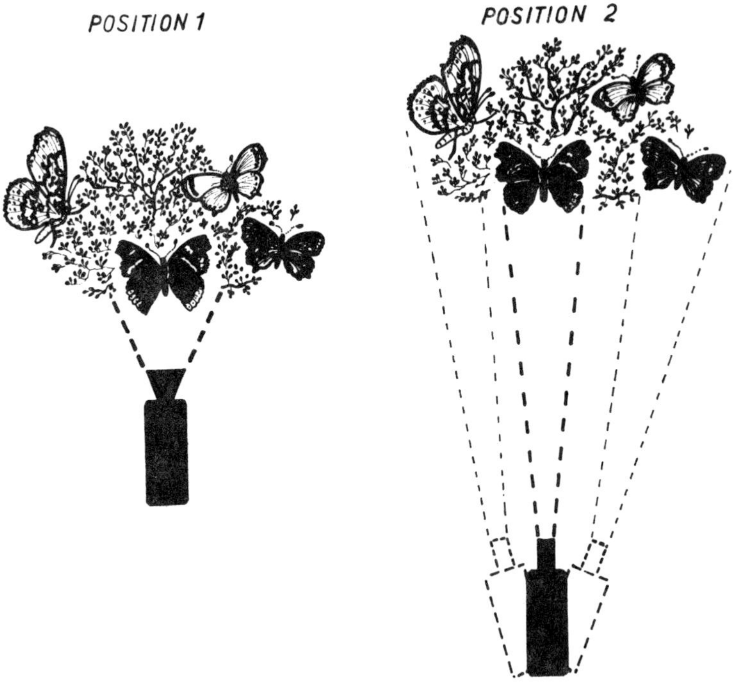

Fig 16 Filming butterflies or other winged insects out of doors

When filming butterflies in this way, or damselflies and dragonflies near a stream, it is worth remembering that such insects often leave a plant only to return a few seconds later to exactly the same position. So once focus has been found on a certain spot it is usually worthwhile to lock the camera position and wait.

Using a 16mm camera to film this sort of shot, a 150mm (6in) lens in conjunction with extension tubes is a fairly satisfactory arrangement; though it is helpful if some sort of sight is mounted on the side of the lens, since it is difficult enough to find focus let alone locate the subject in the reflex viewfinder.

Spiders, and insects that do not fly or move quickly about in grass and foliage, can be filmed with a shorter lens and the camera much closer to the subject. If a slight wind causes movement, it is often possible to provide an effective windbreak over the small area being filmed. This can be improvised with bits of cloth stretched over sticks pushed into the ground, or hung over adjoining bushes. Some cameramen prefer to carry around special Perspex screens which can very quickly be pushed into the ground around the subject (Fig 17). A Perspex cover can be rested across the top of the screens if necessary.

CONTROLLED WORK INDOORS

For good close-up photography of small insects, controlled work indoors is the only satisfactory answer. This is real precision work and only laboratory conditions will do, though the film-maker must ensure that the insects behave quite naturally by providing ideal conditions of vegetation, food, temperature and humidity.

One of the greatest problems in this type of close-up work is how to ensure that these ideal conditions do not vary to any great extent while filming is going on. The most troublesome factor is heat. To get close-ups of good definition with reasonable depth of focus, a lot of light is required. This usually means a lot of associated heat as well, and if precautions are not taken the insect subjects can literally be fried alive within a few seconds.

Nowadays, professionals can avoid this by using a cold

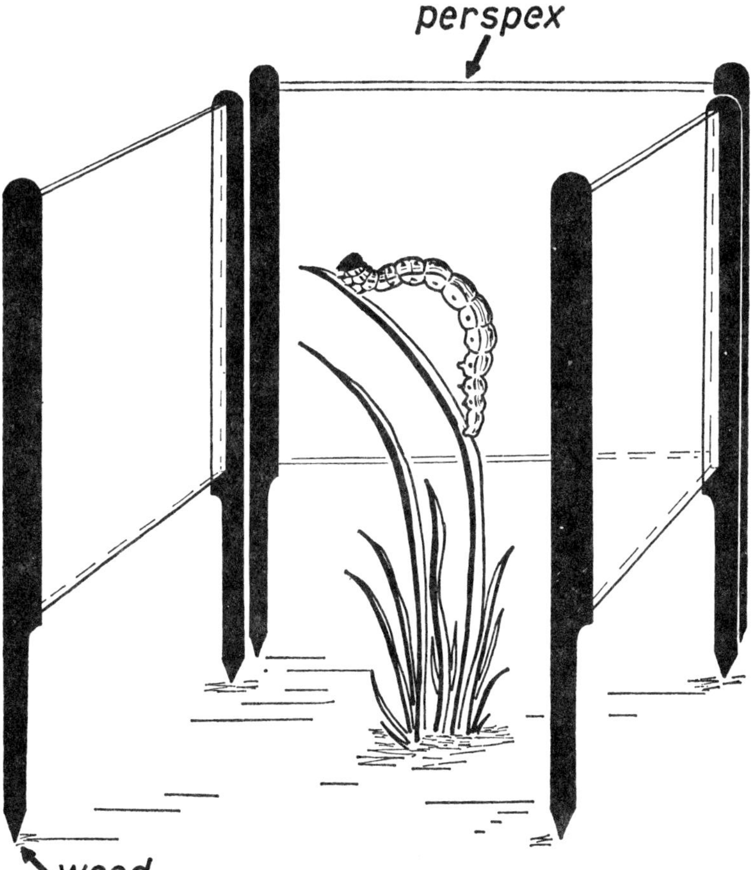

Fig 17 Portable Perspex screens for out-of-doors insect photography

stroboscopic lighting system, where each lamp discharge is synchronized with the camera shutter mechanism, but this is still fairly expensive equipment and probably out of the reach of most amateurs. There are, however, other ways of reducing heat. To my knowledge, the best method so far developed is the lighting system used by Gerald Thompson and Eric

Skinner for their early work on the alder woodwasp (and later modified and improved by Oxford Scientific Films). *The Alder Woodwasp and Its Insect Enemies* is an instructional film, now widely known throughout the world and a British award-winner in 1960. The story of how it came to be made is worth mentioning here if only to give encouragement to beginners. Gerald Thompson and Eric Skinner had only had a few months' experience with the cine camera when they made it, but they were more than halfway to success at the start, for Thompson had a detailed knowledge of the breeding habits of the alder woodwasp and its parasites through his own research work, and he knew what conditions were necessary to induce any given behaviour.

During his research, Thompson had taken a number of close-up photographs of various incidents in the life cycle of the alder woodwasp. On seeing these, Peter Scott encouraged him to repeat them on cine film. Thompson and Skinner acquired a reflex Bolex camera with a 25mm (1in) and a 75mm (3in) lens and some extension tubes, but found it much more difficult to acquire the information they needed to start in this specialized branch of cine photography, known as macro-photography. However, they gradually pieced together scraps of other people's knowledge and experience and finally two essential points emerged:

1 that weighty mountings for subject and camera supports were necessary to cut down vibration
2 that tough glass heat filters must be interposed between lamps and subject.

They immediately set about meeting these requirements, and their success in doing this, coupled with their specialist knowledge of the alder woodwasp, enabled them to complete the desired behaviour sequences in three weeks, a truly remarkable achievement.

SOLUTIONS TO TWO MAIN PROBLEMS

The lighting units used by Gerald Thompson and Eric Skinner for their film are, with some small modifications, the principal form of lighting still employed for macro-work by Thompson and his colleagues. Anyone contemplating this type of filming can do no better than consider the basic elements of these units before designing their own, with appropriate modifications to suit their special needs. The photograph on page 122 shows a number of these units in use, and Fig 18 here gives an exploded diagram of their construction.

The light source is a 240V 500W internal reflector flood, which is mounted inside a copper housing; a brass lamp-holder is used in view of the high temperature. Inside the lamp-housing are fitted two filters of toughened glass (made by Chance Pilkington, England, under the specification HA3), each 3·5mm thick, 5in in diameter, and spaced ½in

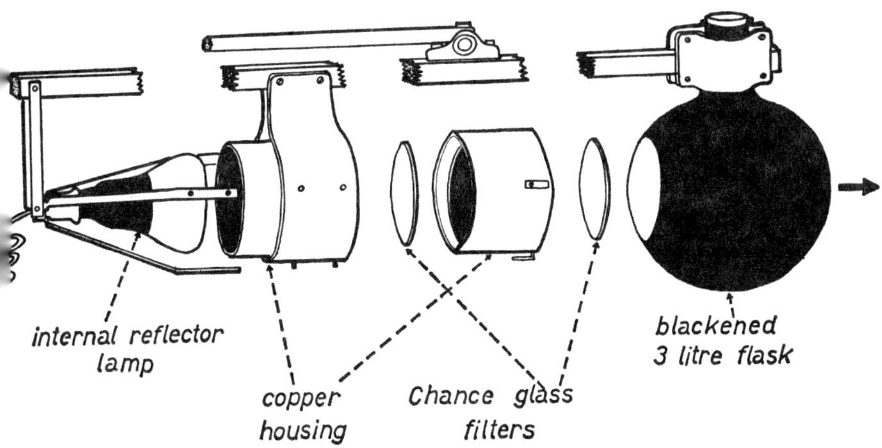

Fig 18 Exploded diagram of lighting unit for insect macro-photography

apart by an asbestos ring. Each filter absorbs about 92 per cent of the heat rays while allowing 86 per cent of the visible light through, and they are the key parts in keeping the subject cool. Since they themselves get very hot, they must be mounted loosely inside the housing to give room for expansion.

The light finally passes through a 3 litre flask filled with distilled water. The purpose of this is not, as may at first be thought, to act as a further heat filter (we have already noted that water is an inefficient method of cooling light), but to act as a simple condenser. The camera field is, at most, likely to be only a few square inches, and the available light must be concentrated on this area; the flask in fact increases the illumination from the lamp by about ten times. It is blackened with blackboard paint except for the light path, and is attached to the same mounting bracket as the lamp, so that the two remain in a fixed position relative to one another.

For very high-power magnifications, for close-ups of insects' eyes for example, much more concentrated light is needed. Special lamps can be constructed for the job, made from a suitable lens mounted in front of a microscope or projector lamp. There are two important points to remember when doing this:

1 check that the lamp gives a light of the correct colour temperature of 3,200K
2 do not tilt a projector lamp at such an angle that it either does not function properly or is damaged

With all cine macro-photography, working in a room with wooden floorboards is asking for trouble. All equipment should rest on solid floors, which may mean using the kitchen (if this is allowed), or better still the basement (if you have one). When filming at actual size (when the image on the celluloid is the same size as the subject) the vibration problem becomes acute, and at magnifications up to twenty times the only answer is to have very heavy equipment indeed. For example, in order to take horizontal shots of magnifications between four times and ten times, Oxford Scientific Films use a camera stand weighing rather more than 300lb and a subject stand of 200lb or so. This kind of set-up is clearly out of the reach of most amateurs, but the specifications help to underline the necessity for steadiness.

Peter Parks, Oxford Scientific Films, has neatly solved the vibration problem when taking dark-ground cine studies of tiny organisms. The subject is mounted on a specially designed optical bench, and can be lit from the rear in such a way that it appears against a dark background. In this case light is transmitted through the subject, but it may also be lit with *incident* light from the front, or indeed a combination of the two. The animal is put in a tiny cell resting on a platform that can be moved accurately in three planes; the camera is fixed rigidly on the end of the same optical bench. This is very important, for then subject and camera, if they vibrate at all, do so in sympathy and to the same extent. This principle is applied here to a particularly sophisticated piece of equipment, but I believe it is one that can be incorporated usefully into the design of less ambitious apparatus.

OTHER PROBLEMS IN MACRO-PHOTOGRAPHY

Many 8mm enthusiasts will be at a severe disadvantage in this field of macro-photography, for detachable lenses and the use of extension tubes are essential for a full range of close-ups. The 16mm reflex Bolex camera with 25mm and 75mm lenses and extension tubes is adequate for up to life-size pictures. For bigger close-ups, lenses of 16mm and 25mm focal length can be used in a reversed position and held by a special adapter of aluminium alloy; at one end is a C-type thread which screws into the camera or extension rings, and at the other, larger, end is a thread that allows it to be screwed into the front of the lens (where the lens cap usually screws on).

Because a large amount of light has to be concentrated on a small area for macro-photography, it is extremely difficult to take an exposure reading in the normal way. Things are further complicated by the extension tubes, the use of which requires more exposure in any case. These exposure compensations become vital as soon as the film image is as large as one-quarter life-size.

There is a formula for determining the increase in exposure:

$$\text{exposure factor} = (\text{magnification} + 1)^2$$

This is all very well if the exact amount of magnification is known. For a given tube or bellows setting, this can be measured by focusing on two dots of known distance apart and comparing the image on the camera viewing screen with the actual width of that screen (10mm for a 16mm camera). If the magnification is found to be 2, then by applying our formula the exposure factor is $(2 + 1)^2 = 9$. In other words, we require nine times as much exposure. Twice as much would be given by one extra stop, four times as much by two extra, eight times by three extra, and for nine times as much exposure, the aperture must be increased by three and a quarter stops. These figures may perhaps help to explain the need for so much light when working at high magnifications, and the corresponding necessity for an efficient heat-filtering system.

For low magnifications the following table may be helpful:

Magnification	*Increase in Aperture*
$\frac{1}{4}$	$\frac{1}{2}$
$\frac{1}{3}$	$\frac{3}{4}$
$\frac{1}{2}$	$1\frac{1}{4}$

1	2
$1\frac{1}{2}$	$2\frac{2}{3}$
2	$3\frac{1}{4}$
3	4

Another method of calculating the correct exposure is to divide the square of the focal length of the lens into the square of the distance between lens and image. (Measure between the film and the position of the lens iris.) If this distance is v, then the increase in exposure is $\frac{v^2}{f^2}$; from this figure you can work out the number of extra stops required. Alternatively, divide the figure given for increase of exposure into the film speed, and reset the meter to the new effective speed.

All these calculations assume that an accurate exposure-meter reading is possible to start with. When it is difficult to calculate an accurate exposure by the use of a meter, an exposure chart for every lens and combination of extension tubes should be prepared. It means using up most of a whole roll of film, but is well worth the initial outlay if there is much of this kind of work to be done. In fact it is the method used by Gerald Thompson and his colleagues for their highly specialized form of macro-photography.

The chart is prepared by exposing the test film roll in bursts of about ten frames at nine half-stop intervals, four exposures below and four above the estimated correct exposure for a given lighting set-up. This is done for every lens and each combination of extension tubes at 5mm intervals. When the test film has been processed and the correct exposure for each combination found, these are tabulated, together with the field size in each case. This exposure chart is valid only for the constant number and position of the lamps used in the tests, so these must be kept the same for all subsequent filming; however, with such a small lit area, this is not a great disadvantage.

As with aquarium filming, it is necessary to have a working light for setting up and focusing while the filming lights are not in use; and this light should be turned off while a shot is being taken if its colour temperature is not the same as that of the filming lights. Although this system is satisfactory for shots taken with ordinary lenses, it is not suitable for high-power magnification requiring a lot of light. Here, the working light may not prove bright enough for focusing, in which case it would be advisable to have the current for all lamps passing through a variac control, or regulator. This can be wound up to a third or a half for focusing, perhaps 100V, and then right up to normal for filming. In this way the insect is subjected to the full intense light for only a short time.

Since most home-made heat-filtering systems are unlikely to be as efficient as Thompson's equipment, it is a wise precaution to keep a careful watch on the temperature: it should not be allowed to rise above 28° C (85° F), except for very short lengths of time.

SETS

Sets are always very small, and in some cases may be no more than a single leaf or part of the bark of a tree. The largest is not likely to be more than 12 × 12 × 12in, for if it is much larger most insects will disappear from view.

The set can be prepared in two ways. A section of soil and vegetation can be dug up with a spade and taken complete to the film studio. Alternatively, the various bits and pieces needed, including plants, twigs and stones, may be collected and assembled in the studio. An old, large rectangular baking tin makes a satisfactory base when a good layer of earth is required for living vegetation that needs daily watering. Once the main set has been prepared, smaller ones for detailed shots can be assembled.

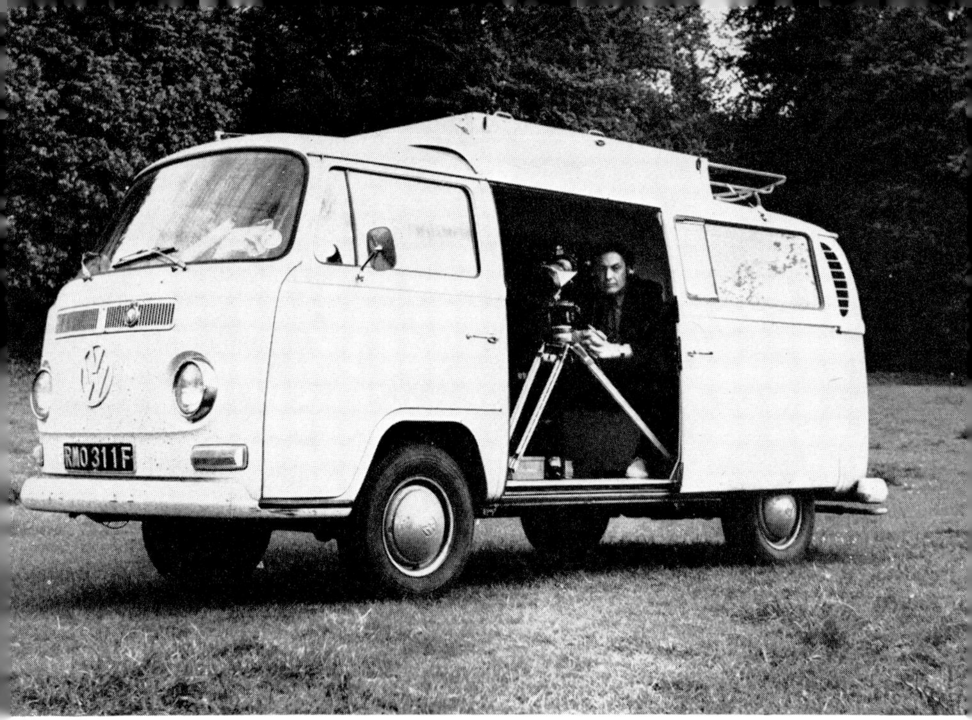

Page 121 (*above*) Type of vehicle particularly suitable for filming birds away from the nest. Normally the side door space is covered with a hide front; (*below*) Ronald and Rosemary Eastman using the vehicle as a mobile hide. The open doorway is covered with a black drape in which a slit has been cut for the lens.

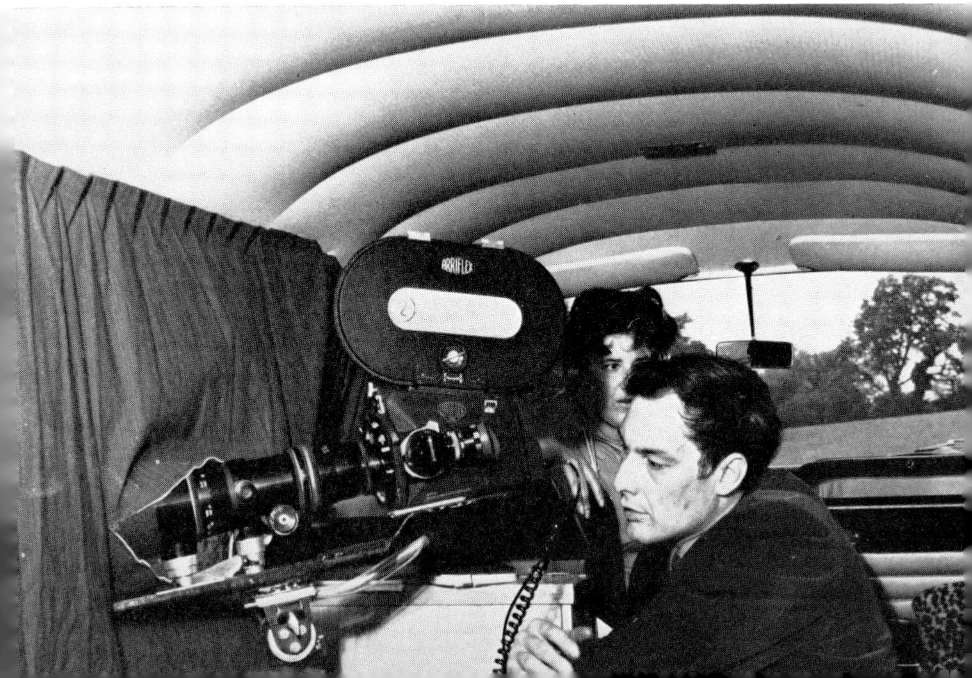

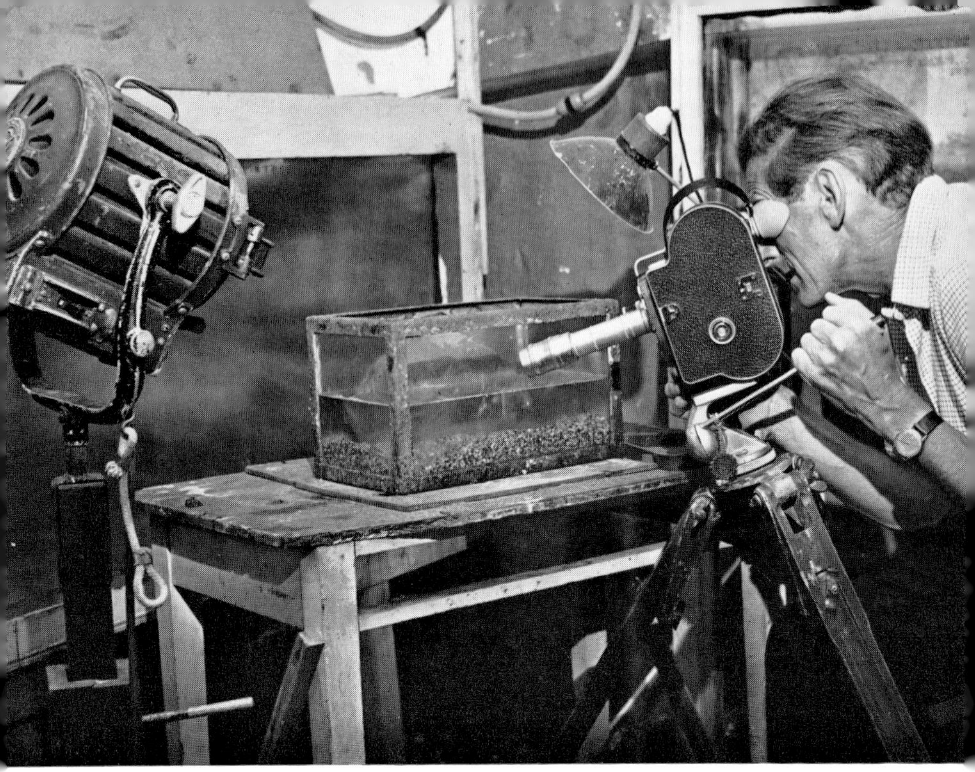

Page 122 (*above*) A table top set-up for filming small freshwater or marine life. The camera here is fitted with a 50mm lens and a 95mm extension tube; (*below*) apparatus used by Gerald Thompson for macro-photography of insects at Oxford Scientific Films. A number of the lighting units drawn in Fig 18 are in use. Note the very heavy camera and subject stand, and the variac control in the foreground.

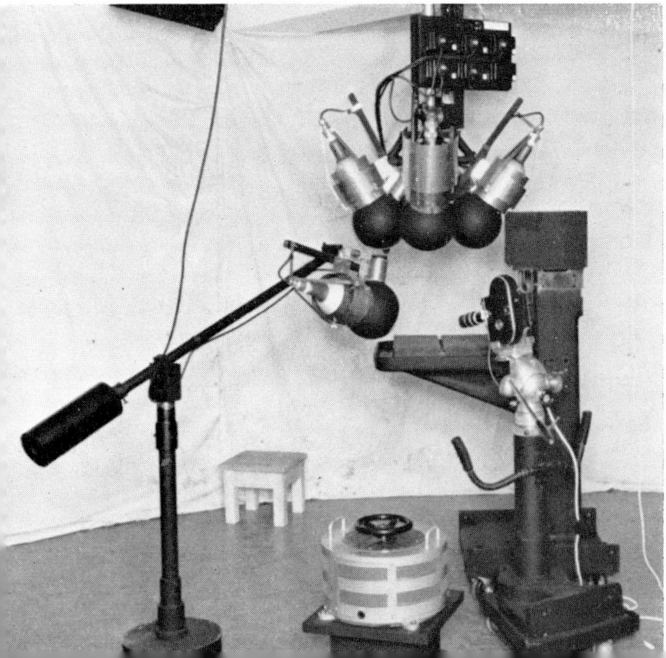

In many cases it is convenient to keep insects and spiders in containers and bring them to the set when filming commences. With slow-moving and non-flying subjects the set may be completely exposed, but for winged insects it must be enclosed in glass or Perspex. When spiders and insects that run about on the ground are being filmed, it is useful to have a moat surrounding the set in order to slow down, if not prevent, escapes.

Sometimes an insect may be required to build a nest, or a spider to spin a web, and for these sequences the subject must of course be kept on the main set. If web building is being filmed then the usual size and position of the web for that particular species must be determined, and the right conditions provided for it in the set, in the best filming position. The set should not be cluttered up with bits of foliage that might make attractive alternative sites for the web.

When Gerald Thompson filmed orb-web spiders he housed them in a collapsible cage made of five pieces of glass, each 2ft × 2ft, built on a light wooden frame and set on a hardboard case. The glass walls and roof were taped together and could easily be removed once the spider had built its web on the filming position. Thompson notes that a high humidity inside the cage seemed to encourage the spiders to spin.

FILMING METHODS

As we have seen, wildlife filming requires thorough research into the life cycle of the subject before ever the camera is brought out; controlled insect and spider macro-photography is no exception. However, if the correct environmental conditions are maintained, the chances of success in this field are rather higher than elsewhere. This is partly because the comparatively short life cycles, often numbered in days, enable the cameraman to be on the spot at key times of metamorphosis, and partly because, being lower forms of life, they seem to be unaware of the human activity going on around them.

Provided the temperature is not allowed to rise above 28° C (85° F) and care is taken to avoid any degree of desiccation, most insects do not seem to take much notice of the brightness of the filming lights. The ones that do will often keep going for the length of time the lights are turned on during a shot, but some difficulty may be experienced with creatures that are either nocturnal or live most of their lives in dark corners. With these, some conditioning is necessary before filming, and this is done by suspending a lamp above their cage or container. Again, care must be taken to see that the temperature does not rise above the danger level.

Another form of conditioning is essential to the successful filming of insect behaviour – the subject must be physiologically ready for whatever action is required. If, for example, an insect is to be filmed feeding, it must be deprived of food beforehand, not just while the camera is being set up but for the period necessary to make it hungry. In the same way virgin males and females kept well apart for a few days will most likely mate quickly when brought together in front of the camera. Even pupation may be delayed to some extent until the right stimulus of a suitable twig, leaf, or a few inches of earth is provided.

For feeding sequences a carnivorous animal may have to be kept off food for two or three days to make it hungry (note that it should never also be thirsty), but even then it is often difficult to film it in the act of catching prey because the action happens very suddenly and quickly. With web-spinning spiders, the prey can be placed in the web but sometimes the spider's reaction is so quick that it will rush to it before the hand is out of shot or the camera even started. So it is always best to start the camera first, and then toss the prey into the web from a little distance. To obtain good close-ups of a spider leaving its shelter and rushing down the signal line or feeling the spirals of the web, try using a tuning fork to stimulate the vibration caused by an insect struggling in the web.

Vegetarian feeders are much easier propositions. The larvae of butterflies and moths feed for hours on end and need not necessarily be kept away from their food plant before filming is started, though it is a good plan to make them hungry to be on the safe side.

With some insects the adult stage is very brief, and mating may take place within a short time of emergence from the pupae. In this case the insects are best obtained in the pupal stage, and the adults allowed to emerge in separate containers. The two sexes are then brought together for the first time in front of the camera. Other species that live in the adult stage for some time before mating can be captured in the field as soon as they make their appearance in spring or early summer. The sexes should then be kept apart, but well supplied with food, for perhaps two or three weeks before mating is filmed.

Gerald Thompson, whose superb films of spiders have been seen by millions on British television, has shown how entertaining these creatures are during courtship. He found that a good courtship performance was more likely with adult spiders caught in the field than with those reared in captivity from a sub-adult stage. He also found that a fairly high temperature sometimes induces courtship, as does the proximity of more than one female.

When an egg-laying sequence is to be filmed, several males and females should be kept in the same cage for several days, care being taken to ensure that they have water and are well fed. Then, and only then, is the correct stimulus for egg laying introduced: this may be a plant, or a piece of dead wood, or some earth, according to the requirements of the particular species.

METAMORPHOSES

One of the most interesting, and photographically most rewarding films for the beginner to make is the life history of a butterfly or moth. If there are only two or three larvae to start with, the chances are that the vital sequences of pupation and the emergence of the imago will take place while the amateur cameraman is otherwise engaged, so it is desirable to have as many larvae as possible, to increase the probability of some of them performing at the right time.

Metamorphoses are not difficult to film, because they take rather a long time. However, thought must be given to the *way* in which they are to be filmed, otherwise there may be problems in editing and one may be faced with a lot of 'jump cuts'. To avoid these, and to enable transitions of time to be made, it is essential to change the camera angle frequently. This should be done with care, so that the big close-ups, which will in themselves be a great aid to editing, will also have some meaning. They should all occur at points where there is a very good reason for going in close: the skin of the larva splitting behind the head as pupation begins, and the head of the imago breaking out of the pupal case, for instance.

Because of the long time some metamorphoses take, cameramen have tried to use a kind of stop-motion technique when filming them. For example, the expansion of a butterfly's wings as the blood is pumped through them after emergence can be filmed by exposing a frame every second. I have always found this unsatisfactory, because from time to time the insect gives a muscular twitch which causes an irritating jump in the shot. I prefer the process to be filmed with greater variety of angle, with the camera running 50 per cent slow.

With fast-moving insects, especially when they are filmed in close-up, there is much to be said for running the camera slightly fast. If normal exposure is 24fps, 32fps will give sufficient difference to make the picture less irritating and yet still give an impression of quick movement. If 18fps is the normal exposure, then 24fps will give the appropriate effect.

9

In Urban Areas

WOULD-BE wildlife film-makers who live in urban areas should not be dismayed if it is difficult for them to make long weekend trips into the countryside in order to pursue their hobby. Aquarium and insect photography may provide possible solutions to their problem: another probably lies right under their noses, in their own gardens.

The variety of animal life that can be found at one time or another in quite a modest-sized town garden is amazing. Many of the smaller garden creatures, such as insects, spiders and other invertebrates, have to be filmed mainly indoors, but at least they are handy to collect, and the establishing scenes and flight shots of butterflies, bees and other insects can be filmed in comparative comfort out of doors. As the small mammals that may be found in gardens are also mainly indoor subjects, most of the really rewarding out-of-doors work in towns is the filming of birds. Here, the film subject can still be controlled to a large extent, for birds can be attracted to a garden in a number of ways.

BIRD-TABLES AND INTELLIGENCE TESTS

The most obvious method of attracting birds to the garden is to provide them with regular supplies of food and water. If one of the main objects is to get good film shots, then the design and position of the bird-table or feeder should be considered carefully. With a small garden, the ideal camera position may well be inside the house, looking out through a window. In any modern house the window glass is probably good enough to permit filming, but in older houses it is often necessary to replace one pane with a piece of plate glass.

The best filming position having been found, the bird-table should then be placed so that big close-ups of, say, a blue tit can be obtained with the longest lens available. At the same time the table must be in good light and near cover. Cover is important, for birds like a few bushes which they can use as an approach path. If these are not already available, then it is well worth planting some and until they are grown a few tall slender branches can be pushed into the ground at strategic points between the bird-table and the nearest growing trees or bushes. These will provide plenty of perching places for birds waiting to get to the table when it is crowded, and will provide useful additional shots to build into a bird-table sequence.

In designing the bird-table, avoid an elaborate construction that gets in the way of the camera, but see that it gives the birds plenty to do. A pile of food on a flat table results in a succession of quick fly-in and fly-out shots, and a lot of greedy gobbling; once a catalogue of all the available species has been compiled the film possibilities are then exhausted.

If, however, a variety of food containers is used, and the food is not always easily removed from them, the birds can be kept at the table long enough for the cameraman to get interesting shots of some of their acrobatic feats. Nuts, bread and other scraps for titmice can be hung up in a small cylindrical cage of wire netting; half a coconut can be hung upside down. A piece of fat suspended on a length of string may lead a blue tit to discover how to perch on the table and pull up the string by putting one foot on the slack at the end of each pull. Once discovered, this behaviour may be

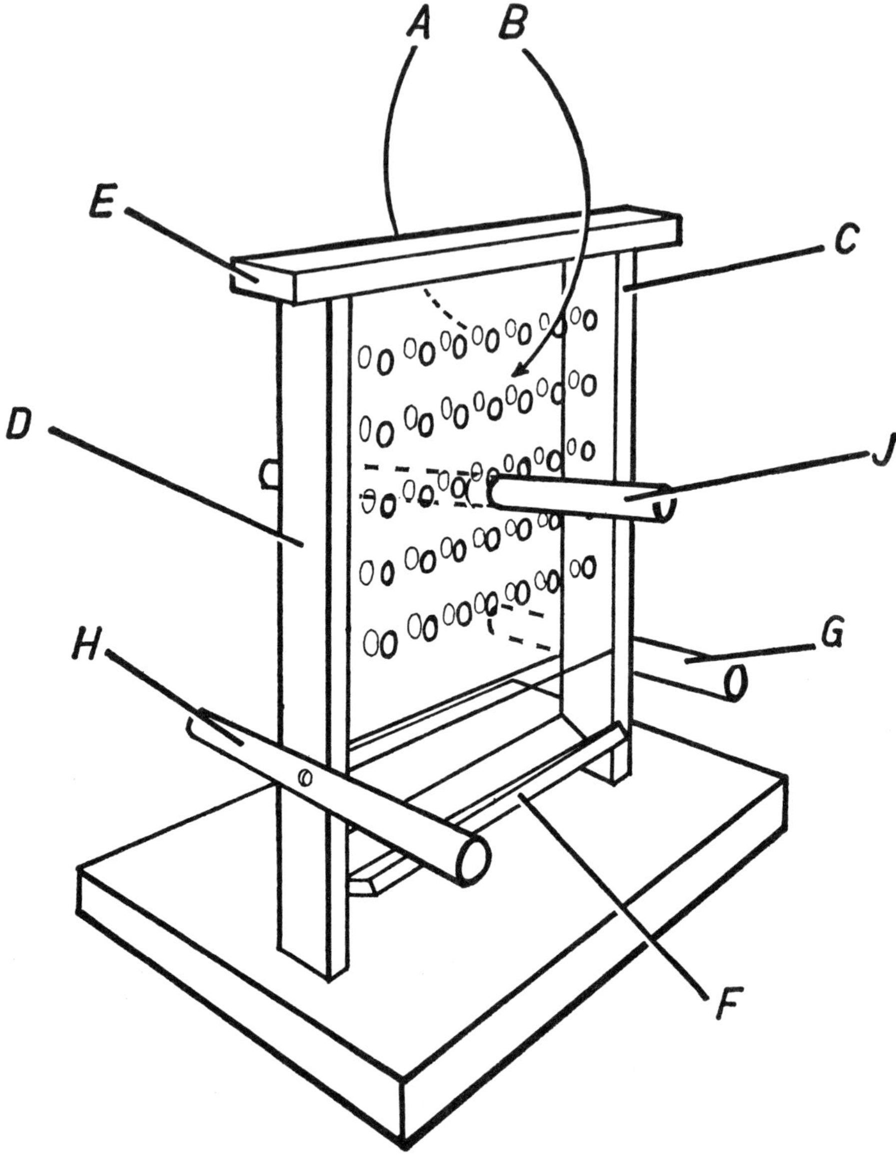

Fig 19 Intelligence test 1 for use on a bird-table

repeated, and this in turn may suggest further ways of testing the intelligence of these birds.

I have twice filmed intelligence tests with tits at a naturalist's bird-table on the edge of Dartmoor, and on each occasion the sequences proved to be of great appeal to television viewers. Two of the experiments are quite easy to set up, and can be constructed as follows.

Two pieces of Perspex, A and B, approximately 8in × 5in, are held ¾in apart by two wooden strips C and D, and mounted vertically on a stand (Fig 19). Several rows of holes are drilled at regular intervals through both Perspex pieces so that matchsticks can be fitted floorboard-wise across the space between. A small roof-piece E fits on the top, and immediately below the Perspex there is a trough F. There are a pair of side perches, G and H, and one central perch J.

The test is set by pushing a few spent matchsticks across through the holes, and then resting a small nut (a shelled peanut will do) between the Perspex sides on two of the matchsticks. The lid is then replaced so that the birds cannot get at the nut through the top.

When the apparatus is first placed on the bird-table it is quite likely that several birds will try to pick at the nut through the Perspex, and if one of the matchsticks is thereby dislodged the nut will fall into the trough where it can easily be recovered. When the test is repeated it is possible that one blue tit will get the idea and pull at the matchsticks to get at the nut. Once this has happened, matchsticks can be inserted in other rows below, so that the bird has to pull at a whole series of them to get the nut. The fascination of filming this behaviour can readily be seen. The only disadvantage is that film consumption will tend to be high because the camera has to be kept running throughout any one bird's attempt.

The apparatus for the second experiment consists of a wooden wheel about 8in in diameter (Fig 20), mounted in a vertical position, with a small test-tube attached to the

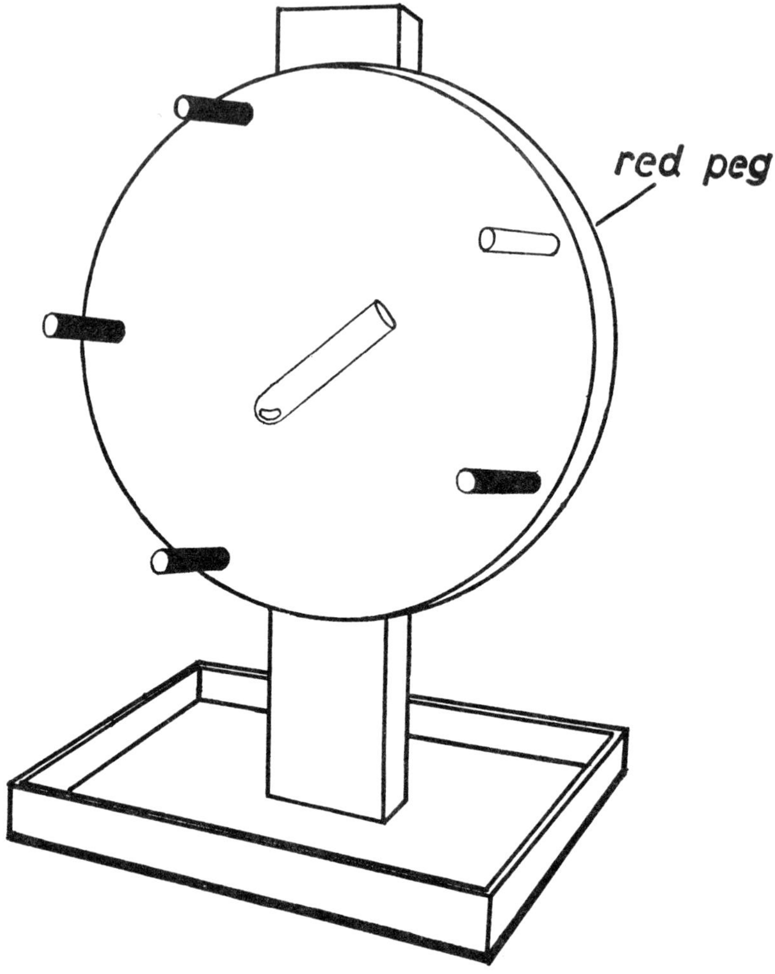

Fig 20 Intelligence test 2 for use on a bird-table

centre. Various perches are screwed into the wheel near the circumference, and if necessary these are weighted so that the contents of the tube are thrown out only when one particular perch is used. This perch is painted red.

The experiment is set up by turning the wheel so that the test-tube is nearly upright, and a nut is then placed in it. Here, too, the reaction of most birds is to try to peck the nut through the glass, but eventually a bird will land on the red perch by chance and up-end the tube. Then it is simply a question of which bird learns first to associate the use of this perch with success in getting the food reward.

The filming of these experiments should be covered mainly by master shots of each bird's attempts, and these should be close-ups in which the whole experimental apparatus fills the frame. There should be no stops and starts within each sequence of a bird's attempt, otherwise the film will have no value as a scientific record. This type of coverage alone, however, will result in a film of jump cuts in which the camera angle never changes, so to make the film presentable additional shots must be taken to join in between the various experiments. These shots should be of the birds and of the experimenter.

In the case of the birds, a different camera position from the main one may be needed in order to get approach shots: flight shots from nearby bushes, establishing shots of them arriving at the table, and closer shots of individuals waiting in the wings, as it were.

Several shots should be taken of the setting up and resetting of each experiment on the bird-table. In the case of the first apparatus, the matchstick positions shown in these shots should correspond with those filmed in the actual experiments.

These sequences are not strictly wildlife filming, for they show an artificial situation not normally encountered by the birds. Nevertheless they do tell us something about the intelligence of wild birds, and so fall into a fringe category which many cameramen may care to include in their hobby.

DOORSTEP, LAWN AND PARK

Many a British housewife has opened the front door in the morning and been irritated to find tha the metal-foil tops of the milk bottles have been pecked at by blue tits and great tits. If the tits are well practised in this activity in the neighbourhood, a fascinating sequence can often be filmed from the comfort of the house. All that is required is the co-operation of the milkman and the forbearance of the housewife.

First of all, arrangements have to be made for milk to be left *regularly* in a position that gives a good camera angle from inside a window. Secondly, the birds must be allowed to continue to peck at the milk-bottle tops prior to filming, in order to maintain their interest. On the day of filming, however, the bottle tops may have to be temporarily covered after delivery until there is light enough for an exposure.

To film birds drinking water is a simple matter: a small shallow bowl on the bird-table is all that is needed. But rather more can be achieved if a small pool, big enough for the birds to bathe in, is provided at the edge of the lawn.

A further aid to the birds' toilet, and a source of yet more film material, is a dust bath. Many birds like to 'powder' themselves in hot dry weather, and they can be encouraged in this pursuit simply by keeping a small area of flower-border free of plants and topped with a layer of very fine earth. Ideally, this should be fairly close to the bird-table and the water bath, so that all three can be covered from the same indoor vantage point.

The lawn is also a source of good action shots. Thrushes and blackbirds searching for worms, then struggling with particularly long and juicy specimens, make splendid and often amusing shots. So does a thrush at his anvil – the stone littered with empty snail shells (and if this cannot be filmed from the house it is worth setting up a hide). Such behaviour is common in many gardens, yet it is rarely observed closely, probably because it is so common. In close-up, these bird activities are among the most popular of all film subjects.

The local park may prove an attractive alternative to the lawn for the sort of film sequences described above. Here the birds are quite used to humans passing by, and the sparrows are often so tame that it is possible to film them dust-bathing from a short distance away without any sort of hide (which is in any case out of the question in a park). A film of this kind was made a few years ago in St James's Park, in the heart of London, by a full television crew – much to the amusement of passers-by.

Perhaps the main attraction of a park like St James's is the lake and its water birds. Many of these birds are ornamental wildfowl, specially introduced to make the place look more attractive; but they are often joined by wild birds, and in winter, in particular, the tame birds serve as decoys to bring in the wild ones. Other species such as moorhen and coot frequently move into parks and are much tamer in these surroundings, allowing nest-building, incubation and feeding of the young to be filmed from an open position quite near.

It should be apparent from the above suggestions that there is a wealth of material for the wildlife film-maker to draw on even in a town or city. A slow accumulation of shots over a year can eventually make an absorbing film about the wildlife of a garden or a park. If filming has to be done mainly in this way, it is well worth making the effort to be up and about on a Sunday morning while other people are lazing in bed. The first few hours of daylight on a fine morning can provide better-than-average opportunities for the cameraman; not only will there be a lot of activity amongst the birds, but sometimes very beautiful effects can be filmed in the early morning mist.

MAKING THE MOST OF A VISIT TO THE ZOO

The filming of tame and captive animals may seem to lie outside the scope of this book, but anyone who has a wide and general interest in animals will want to take his camera to the zoo, and also to film his own pets from time to time. This type of filming is good practice for the beginner and very often an excellent method of learning the basic principles of wildlife photography, so it is worth considering here.

A family outing to the zoo is a favourite subject for amateur cine enthusiasts, but they frequently fail to make the most of it through sheer lack of thought and preparation. Practically every time I visit a zoo I see at least half a dozen cine cameras being used at the wrong time or at the wrong angle.

Some form of planning and reconnaissance is a requisite of any film, and a zoo film is no exception. A preparatory visit should therefore be made, before the camera and the family are taken along. Although good close-up studies of animal faces provide a valuable ingredient in the film, remember that animals make the best cine pictures when they are engaged in some sort of activity. Do not plan to photograph animals in old-fashioned cages with small mesh wire or close bars. Go for those in open paddocks, enclosures surrounded by moats, and outdoor cages with at least one side of glass; glass-fronted indoor cages are likely to prove difficult because of the lack of light. Having decided on the best animals to film, the next thing to discover is their feeding times. The feeding of such animals as penguins, sea lions and bears can usually be guaranteed to give good action shots, and these may well provide the visual climax of the film.

Some thought should then be given to the best camera positions for filming. All too often I have seen someone with a cine camera walk up to an enclosure, and almost in one movement put the camera viewfinder to his eye and shoot a few seconds of film. This is pouring money down the drain. So often the cameraman has only to walk to the other side of the enclosure to get a closer position and a steadier shot, and quite possibly better angles. Where complicated action sequences are involved, as in the feeding of sea lions, these should be covered by shooting from several different camera angles.

In addition to one or two main-action sequences in a zoo film, it may be desirable to add shorter sequences in order to show the range of animals in the collection. If it is necessary to shoot some of these through ugly wire netting try to view the subject through one of the holes in the mesh. Where this is not possible, the distracting effect of the netting can be minimized by shooting from farther away, preferably with the camera on a tripod. If the animal is a little way from the fence when photographed, the wire will be slightly out of focus and appear as a faint grey blur. This can be tolerated for short sequences, especially if the animal is engaged in some interesting activity, and may be better than not having the animal on film at all. It is a method that works best when the sun is not out, for on dull days the camera operates at a large lens aperture and therefore with less depth of focus; this makes it easier to get the fence out of focus.

Having made careful preparations the cameraman can then feel free to make the most of opportunist shooting, both of animals and visitors. Amusing and spontaneous reactions between a child and an animal have to be filmed surreptitiously and 'off the cuff'. Some establishing scenes are also needed: wide-angle shots showing the gardens and the movement of visitors from one part of the zoo to another.

PRACTISING ON PETS

Anyone who thinks that the filming of pets is simple is in for a surprise. No animals, wild or domesticated, can be directed like a human being. A trained animal like a dog can be commanded to carry out a number of basic actions; but other and more complex actions result from certain conditions and stimuli and can only be filmed by patiently waiting for them to occur, or by arranging to provide them.

Take a simple example: a close-up is required of a dog drinking from its water bowl. The dog cannot drink to order; it will only drink when it is thirsty. However, a romp in the park or garden usually makes a dog thirsty, so this has to be arranged. If possible, someone else should exercise the dog and prevent it from drinking before filming starts. In the meantime, the cameraman has an opportunity to set up his camera and install lights.

Even with this kind of planning there may be difficulties. If the dog is not already accustomed to the camera, it may be nervous or inquisitive. Ideally it should have been conditioned to accept the camera and its noise, the lights, and all the other associated filming paraphernalia. Much depends on the individual animal, but generally speaking the greater the thirst the less danger there is of the dog being distracted by the film equipment. It will go straight for its bowl and the cameraman films his sequence.

Domesticated animals, like wild ones, have a regular daily pattern of behaviour, and filming them is likely to be successful if this routine is respected. For example, a sequence may be required of a kitten playing with a favourite toy: a rubber mouse or a piece of paper tied on a string. First of all, the plaything should be kept away from the kitten for some time, perhaps twenty-four hours, before filming. Then the choice of time for filming is particularly important; it is no use

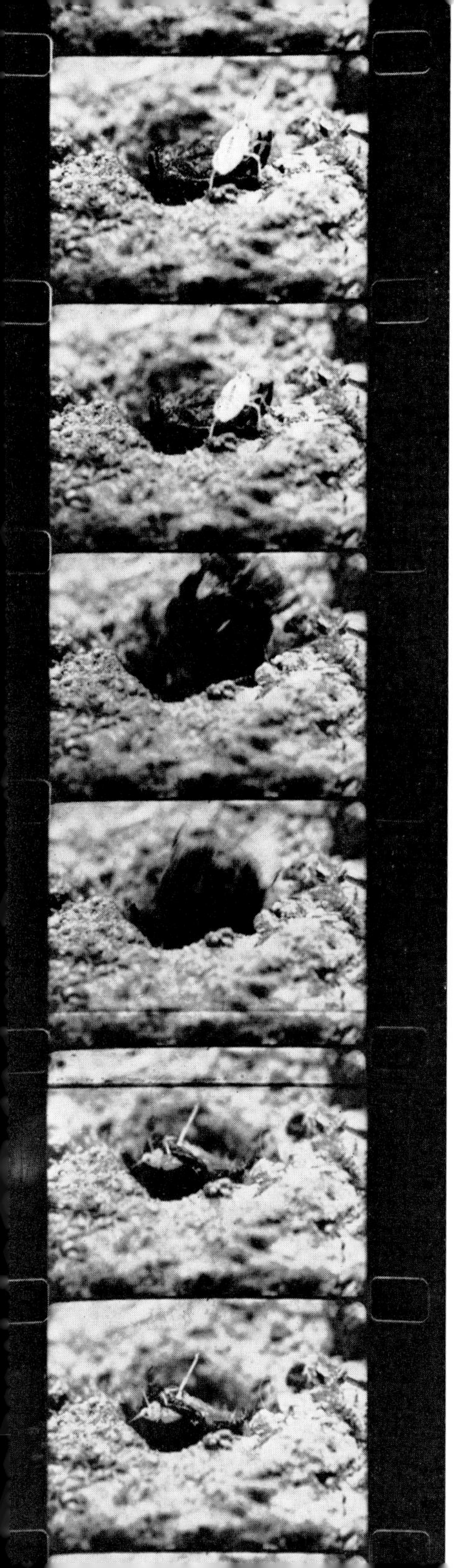

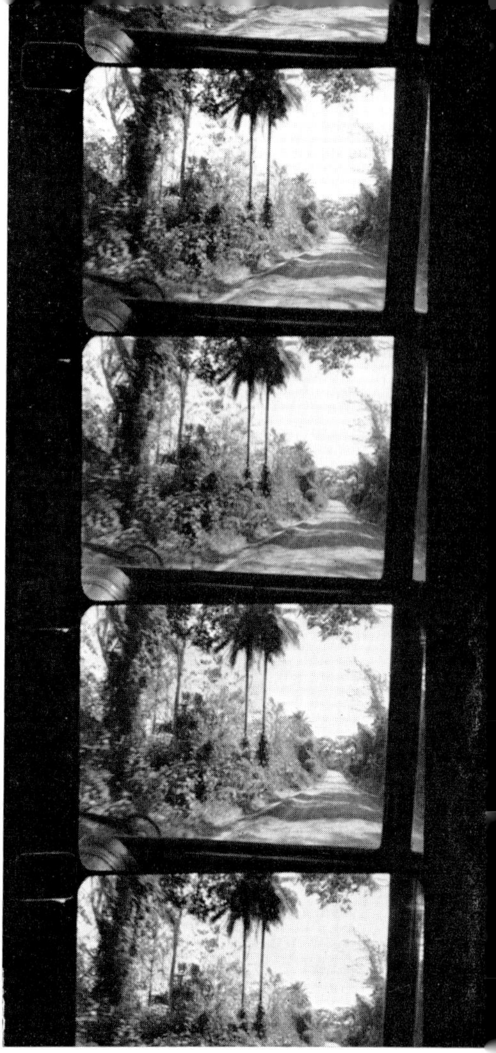

Page 139
(*left*) Avoiding a jump cut. The fast movement of insects sometimes makes this possible as shown in this frame sequence from *Look – Tiger Beetle*. In the first four frames a tiger beetle larva (only its head is above ground) is seen catching an aphid. Although the shot that immediately follows is almost identical, the cut is not noticed because it occurs at the end of a very fast action which takes up most of the screen; (*above*) a tracking shot from a vehicle on a bumpy road. The camera is made rigid with respect to the chassis, part of which appears in frame and is stable, thus ensuring a shot of acceptable smoothness.

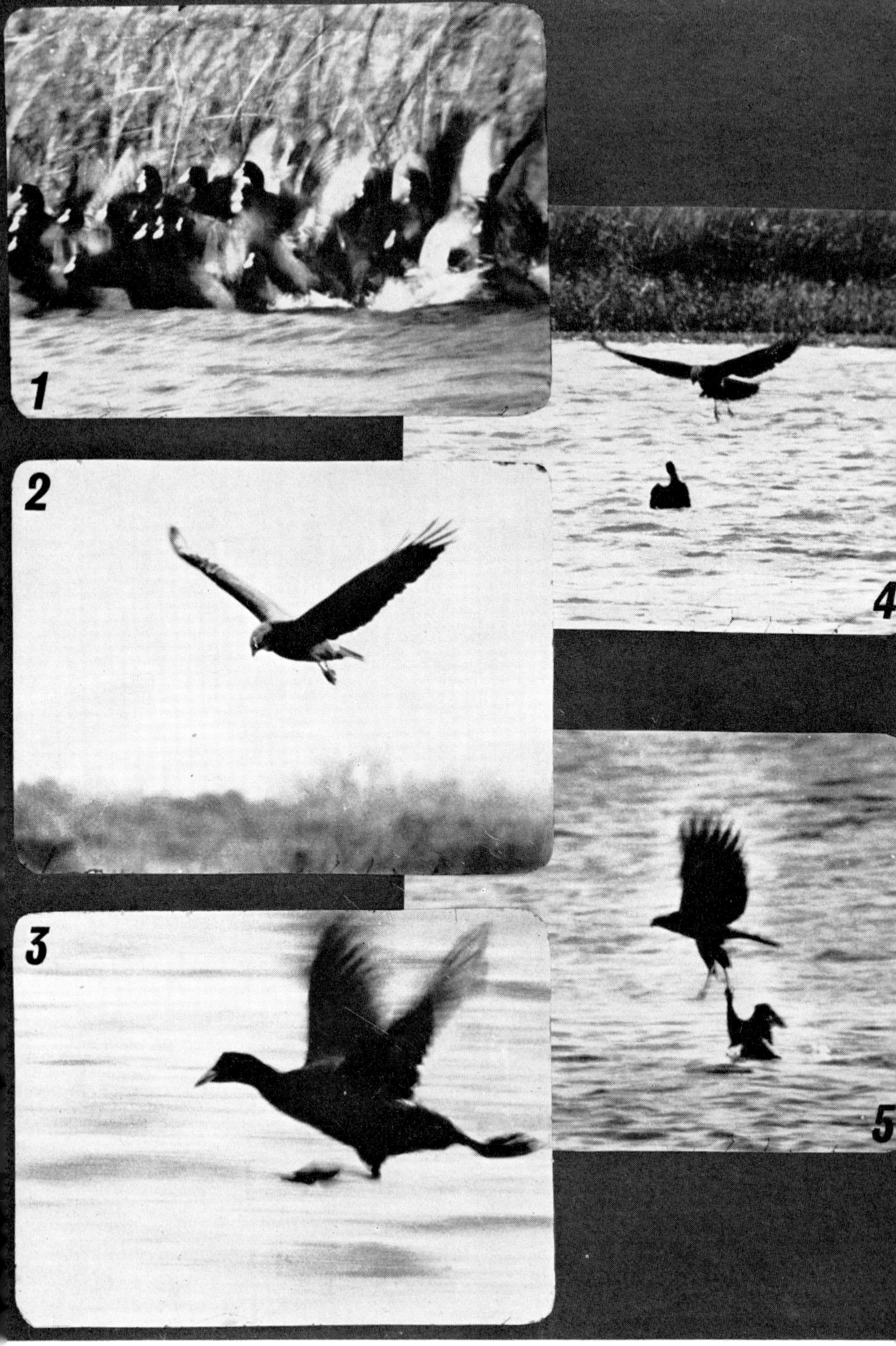

Page 140 Opportunist filming: a sequence that could not possibly have been planned or predicted. A marsh harrier panics a group of coot into taking cover near the reeds. One straggler is left behind to face a long battle with the harrier, until it is eventually too weak to dive or peck back, and is finally lifted bodily out of the water.

trying to get the kitten to play in the early afternoon if this is usually its time for sleep. If its most playful time is in the evening, then this is the time to have the camera set up.

The filming of pets also gives the cameraman useful experience in the choice of camera angles. In wildlife work camera angles are largely determined by circumstance, but where a choice is possible the difference between two camera angles can be the difference between a very ordinary shot and a very striking one. The graceful leap of a gazelle is best photographed with the camera quite low and the animal running at right angles to it; the movement of some snakes is best shown by filming them from almost directly above.

It is particularly important with most small animals, however, that the camera should be *at their level*, if at all possible. Studies of a cat drinking milk or a kitten playing with a ball will be much more attractive on the screen if the camera is placed almost at floor level. The camera can probably be made sufficiently steady by resting it on a couple of heavy books while the cameraman lies out behind it, flat on his stomach. Good camera angles are very often achieved only by suffering some personal discomfort!

Practice in angle-getting can be further extended by filming more active sequences, such as the exercising of a dog. On more than one occasion I have watched a ball-retrieving sequence being filmed. The cameraman stands in one position (Fig 21) without moving a foot during the shooting of the entire sequence; a friend repeatedly throws the ball and the dog repeatedly retrieves it. The results, I fear, must make the audience dizzy, for the camera is continuously panning backwards and forwards.

This distressing effect could have been avoided had the two basic camera positions A and B been used (Fig 22). Here the action takes place diagonally towards and away from camera, and little or no panning is necessary. Moreover, the camera angle can be widened or narrowed to vary the shot

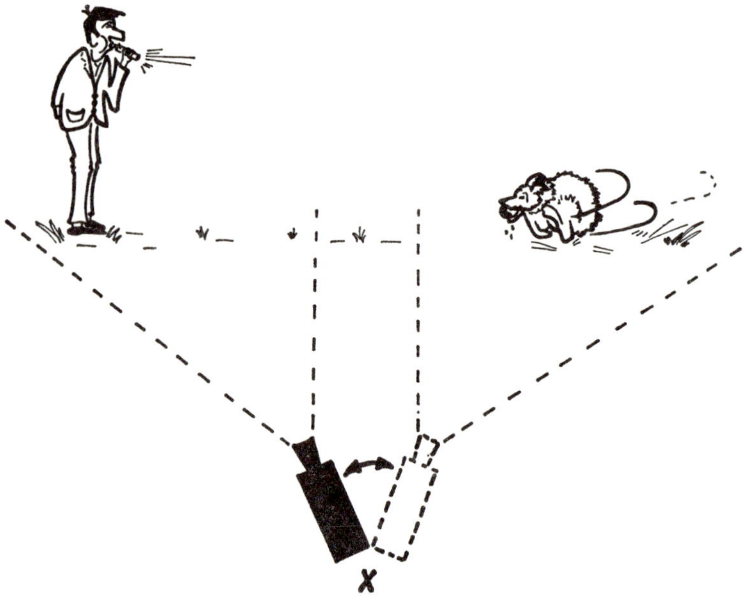

Fig 21 Poor camera angle for filming man and dog

from each position. For example, a medium wide-angle shot can be taken from A with the human on the left-hand side of frame and the dog moving on the right. This can be shot from normal tripod height, or hand-held from a standing position. A closer shot of the dog arriving with the ball and waiting for it to be thrown again can be obtained by crouching low with the camera hand-held. Similar angles can be found for the second part of the action from B, with the dog running up into the foreground and the human in the background.

Use of these two main camera angles does not necessarily mean that nothing at all should be shot from the original camera position X. Indeed, a few shots from there can give a good impression of the dog's speed and exuberance, and provide another agreeable change of angle. They will be best achieved from a tripod (provided it has a smooth pan head), using a lens of medium focal length. If the lens angle is too wide, the dog will be small and trees and other objects will appear to be whizzing by. The lens should be narrow enough to exclude background trees and other objects on the skyline, so that the dog will be seen against a background of grass only and will occupy a good proportion of the complete frame. The effect of speed can then be shown against a blur of green grass, which will not be distracting so long as the cameraman is able to follow the movement of the dog smoothly and keep it consistently framed.

This is excellent practice in camera operation, and is valuable even if no film is run through the camera. For the ambitious cameraman who plans to move into the more advanced field of filming truly wild animals, a few hours spent following dogs and seagulls in the viewfinder will probably save many future disappointments, and many an expensive length of film.

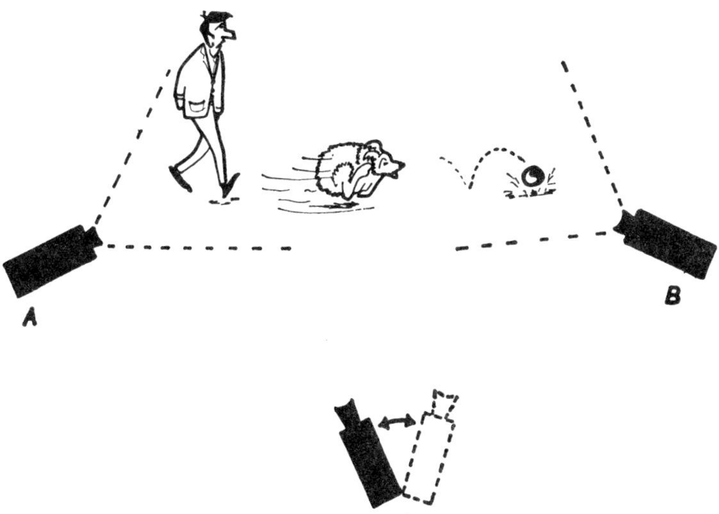

Fig 22 Better camera angles for filming man and dog

10

Build-up Sequences

A FILM that is no more than a succession of medium and close shots can easily turn out to be boring, however interesting the animal action may be. Without any establishing wide-angles and long shots, much important, perhaps vital, information may have been omitted. Such films are not likely to command the viewer's attention for long, because he does not know the setting for much of the subject material and instead of enjoying an *experience* he finds himself just watching pictures.

In many wildlife films the actual content of true wildlife shots may be 60 per cent or less. The remainder most probably consists of establishing shots of habitat, linking action shots involving humans on scientific work or travel, with atmospheric mood material to convey the changing of a season or time of day. In their own way, all these can be used to change the pace and the mood of a film, and provide a setting for the real 'jewels', which are the hard-earned natural history sequences.

Unfortunately, all too often this build-up material is filmed last, in a hurry, and with little thought. In fact, just as much care ought to be given to these shots as to the filming of the animals: they can almost double the value of the wildlife sections of the film and turn a series of interesting shots into a piece of real film-making.

ESTABLISHING SCENES

When filming any sequence, the one question the cameraman should keep asking himself is, 'Will the audience know where we are?' To make quite sure that it will, some establishing scenes may be necessary to show the type of habitat: in the simplest case, perhaps one or two wide-angles nicely composed with the aid of a few foreground bushes or a branch of a tree. But care must be taken to ensure that these scenes are not boring. In a wood or by a stream it may be possible to compose a really beautiful picture of great visual interest, but in an open field this may not be so easy. Some action within frame is therefore desirable, and this should be of some relevance to the sequence that follows: a bird flies towards camera from afar and lands a short distance from its nest-site, or a distant group of animals is seen walking up to a water-hole.

Sometimes it is impossible to include any action at all on a bare landscape; sometimes a particularly desolate scene may be required to convey a certain mood. In these instances something else has to be found to give the scene a touch of visual interest and to provide scale. A large reed bed makes a dull picture if the bottom half of the frame is entirely reeds and the top half entirely sky; but part of a willow on one side of frame will greatly help the composition. Bits of driftwood and broken gates in the foreground would serve a similar purpose and also give depth to the picture.

Large expanses of mud and water can pose problems for the photographer, though there may be a few clumps of reeds, an old boat, or even a few rotten posts to help. In this situation establishing shots should not be filmed when the sun is high or behind the camera. Back-lighting is preferable, for it helps to emphasize the ripples on the water and the patterning of the mud in a way that is visually attractive and emotively compelling.

There is no great virtue in composing a picture with a level horizon exactly halfway down the frame, especially in very flat country (Fig 23, top). A better composition is usually achieved with foreground land or water occupying about the lower two-thirds of frame, and sky the remainder. Foreground land or water filling the lower third of frame, or even less, can also make a well-composed picture, but here a particularly attractive sky pattern is essential, either cumulus clouds or a good sunset or dawn (Fig 23, bottom). Either of the above compositions can be used to give an effect of wide-open space.

USE OF PANNING IN BUILD-UP

It may sometimes be necessary to use a panning movement to convey a whole scene in one film shot. This raises some very important points of procedure. Firstly, the camera should be static for a second or two at the beginning and end of the pan. When editing, it is generally unsatisfactory to have to cut in and out of the middle of a moving pan shot, except in special circumstances (such as an intercut with a close-up of a man scanning the horizon). Therefore static sections at the beginning and end of the pan are desirable, even though the film editor may eventually trim the shot to within a few frames of the start or end of the camera movement.

Each of these static sections should be long enough to be used as separate shots, for when the editing stage is reached it may be found that the pan itself is too long. The beginning and end of the pan should therefore be carefully composed. The cameraman would be wise to rehearse the pan several times without using any film to ensure that he can judge when to ease the camera into its final framing.

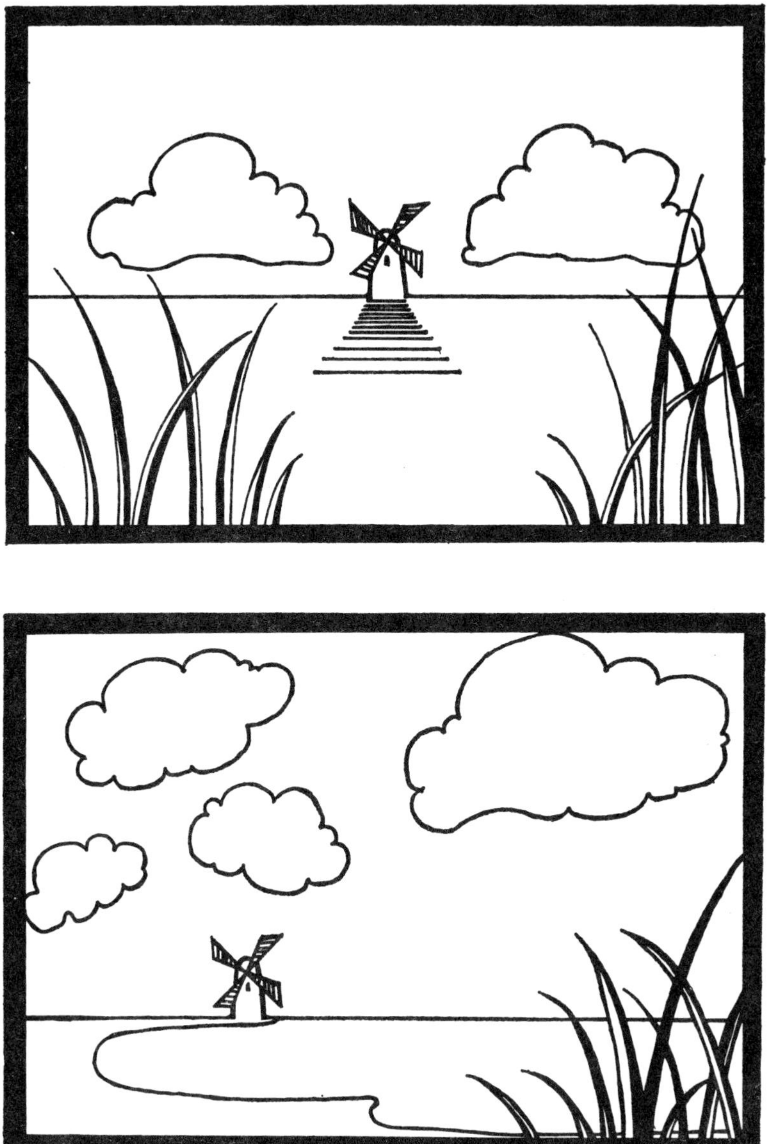

Fig 23 Compositions of flat, open scenes

Care should also be taken to make sure that the pan is not too fast: it is better to imagine the whole picture projected onto a large screen as one looks through the viewfinder than to consider the movement of the camera as just a physical operation. Panning is usually best done with medium wide-angle lenses (16mm or 25mm on a 16mm camera); if an extremely wide-angle lens is used, severe distortion may be seen on both sides of the screen, and objects such as buildings and trees will appear to change shape as the camera moves over them.

Whenever possible, something in the field-of-view at the beginning of the pan should be found to motivate the camera movement. A bird in flight moving left to right may look very small, but it gives a good excuse for panning in the same direction, even though the pan may not be able to follow the pace of the bird. A boat on an estuary may provide a similar motivation. But in these general establishing shots it is best that such moving objects are not close to camera, otherwise they will be thought to be significant to the story.

Where several wide-angle shots are needed to lead into a sequence, there should not be too many pans. They use up a lot of film, are time-consuming, and more than one or two in a sequence of half a dozen shots can become tedious.

ZOOMING WITH DISCRETION

The value of the zoom lens lies in its great variety of focal length within a given range, so that action can always be framed comfortably even though the distance of the subject from the camera may vary considerably. It also has some uses in the shooting of build-up material, but it should always be used sparingly; too many zooms are as bad as too many pans.

A zoom shot is sometimes used to combine a wide-angle establishing shot with a medium shot. By zooming in while the camera is running, the subject can be 'found' in its natural habitat. This is particularly effective with animals that are well camouflaged. For example, an incubating ground-nesting bird can be filmed with the zoom lens at its widest so that it is practically impossible to distinguish bird from background; then, by slowly zooming in, the bird gradually becomes visible, and the effectiveness of its camouflage is thus emphasized. The same kind of shot can be used for just the nest and eggs, which are often even more difficult to see. The same point about camouflage can be made by delaying the zoom shot until the end of the sequence and then using a zoom-out.

Zooming out can in fact be very dramatic, and is particularly effective in creating a feeling of loneliness when used on a single human or animal in a very large open area with little vegetation. At first the figure is seen in medium long shot, filmed with the zoom lens at its longest focal length; then a slow zoom back (but not too slow) reveals the entire area. This movement of the zoom lens relates the size of the lone figure to the vastness of the surrounding area much more impressively than does the straightforward use of the wide-angle shot.

There was a time when convention demanded that practically every new sequence within a film had to start with a fade-in and end with a fade-out. Transitions from one location to another and passages of time were nearly always denoted by dissolves, where one shot mixed directly into the next. Although still useful on occasion, these film effects, or 'opticals', are now out of fashion. Cinema audiences are quite used to ruthless and direct cutting between different locations, and from one period of time to another. However, the audience is usually given some clue at the beginning of a new sequence, either visually or in the dialogue or commentary, which enables it to follow the story. Visually, this information may be given in the first close shot opening the sequence, and sometimes a zoom lens is used to follow the action out from the close-up. This device is extremely useful for wildlife films, especially those that follow an animal or group of animals through the seasons. Where it is necessary to start a sequence in a new season, or to move the action on at least a month or two, a hard cut to a key close-up followed by a zoom-out will often do the trick.

For example, in a woodland film there may be a sequence showing deer activity, perhaps the rut in autumn. The next scene is two months later when the deer are in another part of the wood near a stream. This sequence could be introduced by a shot starting close on icicles overhanging the water, then widening to the whole woodland scene, and the transition is made smoothly. This may involve the use of both zooming and panning in order to make good picture composition in the last part of the shot, so a good tripod head is desirable, and several rehearsal runs should be made before any film is actually taken.

TRACKING SHOTS

There are occasions when part of a journey has to be filmed to show story build-up in a wildlife sequence. When the journey is done by car or Landrover a nice sense of travelling is achieved by the use of tracking shots, in which the camera takes the driver's or passenger's viewpoint and records the changing scenery.

Tracking shots are often difficult to take successfully. This is frequently blamed on bumpy road conditions, but in fact it is nearly always because the camera has been hand-held in those conditions. Hand-held tracking shots should only be attempted if the vehicle has good suspension and is travelling over very smooth road surfaces, otherwise some other method of filming has to be found. Fortunately the solution is quite simple, but is the opposite of what most cameramen usually do. The camera has to be made absolutely rigid in respect of the chassis of the vehicle. Ideally it should be bolted to the chassis in some way, but as this is nearly always impracticable a compromise has to be made. The camera is mounted on a tripod and this is strapped and tied very securely to the floor, seats or whatever rigid fittings are available. The tripod position cannot usually be varied very much because of the layout of the vehicle. Tripod legs may indeed have to be jammed between seats, but this can help towards rigidity. Provided the driver is free to manoeuvre, the other occupants of the vehicle, including the cameraman, may have to put up with some discomfort during the filming operation.

Tracking shots must be filmed on a wide-angle lens if they are to appear smooth, and each shot should be framed so that part of the bonnet or hood, or at least the edge of the windscreen appears in it. This part of the vehicle always appears steady in shot provided the camera is fixed rigidly, and even though the vehicle may be bumping and rocking quite violently, the shot will still be acceptable on the screen. By using this method, I myself have obtained satisfactory results from a Landrover driven over a track of stones and boulders that looked more like a dried-up river bed than a road.

Several tracking shots all taken from the same angle will not cut together without jump cuts. If the sense of a long journey is to be conveyed, additional camera angles will be needed, including various passing shots along the route, and for these the camera has to be set up at the side of the road and sections of the route retraced. Additional useful shots as, for example, of the driver and passengers can be filmed from inside the vehicle.

HUMAN ACTION

Even in films that are basically about wildlife there are sometimes good reasons for the presence of human characters, particularly if the film has a conservation theme. Such sequences are often planned carefully, but the cameraman used to filming only wild animals sometimes forgets that humans can be rehearsed. It is also possible to break up the action into the ideal individual shots, such as long shots for setting the scene and establishing neighbouring birds or animals, and medium and close shots for important action.

Suppose, for example, that a sequence is required of an ornithologist carrying a short ladder to a tree where there is a nest-box fixed some twelve feet up the trunk. The man rests the ladder against the tree, climbs up and takes the lid off the box to look inside and check the number of eggs in the nest.

This sequence could be filmed in three shots. The first, taken from ground level, might be a long shot of the man arriving at the tree, setting up the ladder and climbing two-thirds of the way up it. The second could be a closer shot of the man climbing further up the ladder and lifting the lid off the nest-box; this could be filmed from ground level or from higher up the tree looking down on the man. The third shot could show the interior of the nest-box as the lid is lifted off and replaced.

There are a number of important points to be remembered when shooting such a sequence. The first is continuity. The man must handle the ladder in exactly the same way in the first two shots. If he climbs with his hands holding the uprights in the first shot, he must do so in the second shot also; it would be wrong if he held onto the rungs instead. If the sequence has to be filmed over a period of more than one day, it is also important to check that the same clothes are worn.

It is important to make sure that the action is always in the correct direction. If the man walks left to right in the first long shot, then he must continue in the same general direction, in respect of the camera, in the second. If this second shot is at a high angle from up the tree, then the man climbing up towards camera should come slightly from the left.

Failure to be consistent about direction results in a bad cut when the film is edited, and the audience may even momentarily think that it is looking at a different person.

Yet another requirement is that the action should overlap in each shot. In the first long shot the camera follows the man from ground level to two-thirds of the way up the ladder. In the second shot the action should be taken up from a point at least halfway down the ladder, so that there is an overlap between the two shots. If the second shot shows the complete action of taking the lid off the nest-box, then in the third shot the removal of the lid is repeated; the action could start close on the top of the box with the man's hand coming into frame. The replacement of the lid and the complete withdrawal of the hand out of shot would give a satisfactory end to the sequence. If the shot runs on for a second or two, the slight extra length to the scene will enable it to be followed by almost any action in any location.

The above sequence could be improved by other additional coverage. For example, the close-up of the lid being removed may not fully reveal the eggs inside, and a big close-up may be needed. Also, an intercut of the adult birds waiting to return to their nest could be effectively used as a brief insert.

11

Scripting

THE short days of winter bring fewer opportunities for wildlife filming, but time can always be well spent in preparing special equipment and in research and scripting for the next season's work.

COMPROMISE AND MODIFICATION

Very few wildlife films can be scripted to the extent of writing down every scene in advance of shooting, since animal behaviour and climatic conditions are much too uncertain. One cannot be sure, for example, two months before shooting of being able to film a robin nesting in an old kettle (though the chances of doing so could be increased by advanced planting of old kettles in robin territories). Again, an amateur cameraman on a one-day trip into the Serengeti National Park in Tanganyika *might* have the extreme good fortune to film a lion making a kill, but neither he nor even a professional film crew on a two-week assignment could *expect* this. It would be useless to script such specific sequences into the main action of a film. But it would be equally foolish to start shooting a film without first committing *some* course of action to paper. Between these two extremes lies a necessary compromise.

My own working method usually starts with the setting-out of the film story I am aiming at, but incorporating only sequences that I am reasonably sure of getting. The arrangement of sequences is determined mainly by the story-line, but it may be modified later by the need to place the film high-spots at key positions. The most memorable sequence, the film's climax, must come near the end, but the film also has to open with a particularly arresting sequence in order to involve the audience right from the start. (This is particularly important in television films, where the audience can either switch off or turn to another channel.) Other high-spots are spaced at judicious intervals between the beginning and end of the film. Careful thought about the position of these key sequences is important, otherwise all the best material may appear in the first half of the film and the rest just trails to an end in anticlimax and boredom.

Usually the high-spots of the film are action sequences which require little or no commentary. The intermediate sequences, consisting largely of build-up material, carry all the information, so I often write a draft commentary in note form for these as a guide to the number or length of scenes to be shot. At the same time I make notes about bonus sequences that might be filmed if fate is kind to me. The following is part of my workscript for a film about the Camargue region in the south of France.

Action	*Notes*
Very calm weather scenes – reflection of clouds in water – lakes as smooth as mirrors	Some days are so still one can hardly believe it is winter.
First ripples over still water	The mistral starts very gently, taking you unawares. Then drops and rises, and
Windmill starts to turn	finally screams across the
Horses restless, manes in wind	marshes, freezing everything and making everyone irri-
Reeds bowing in wind	table.

Action	*Notes*
Various birds, mainly duck, landing, and keeping near reed-beds	
Water choppy, frothy Birds on rough water Windmill turning furiously	(a gradual sound build-up after end of commentary prologue)
Huddles of birds	
Solitary bird landing	
Large expanse of reed-bed in wind	
Very rough water	
Groups of birds on and out of water near reeds	(sound subsides a little)
Marsh harrier appearing over reed-beds	As soon as the wind is manageable the harriers are out again.
Ideally, harrier panicking birds and taking prey	(will depend on good fortune)

This is the kind of basic filmscript to aim for before filming starts, although it is bound to be modified several times during the course of shooting, depending on successes and failures and whether or not something unexpected turns up. There may, for example, be some unusual predator action or freak weather conditions just too good to leave out of the film. Some sequences, on the other hand, may appear to be quite straightforward on paper but will eventually prove impossible to film for one reason or another. Part of the skill of making a wildlife film is the ability to modify the script to accommodate changes in fortune. This means a re-assessment of work at the end of almost every day's shooting.

There may be occasions when a 'gift' sequence cannot be used in the film without upsetting the original story. If this is so, there is nothing to do but to put it to one side and hope to incorporate it in another film at a later date. But good and bad luck can change the emphasis in a film without completely altering its basic shape or changing its message. Suppose, for example, that in a film being made about marsh life one of the birds is being covered in some detail in order to give the film a central character. After several weeks' work there may have been a number of serious failures with this 'star' character, but an extremely lucky sequence has been filmed of another common species. If this is an exciting and unusual action sequence, it may be worth considering interchanging the roles of the two species and relegating the original 'star' to a subsidiary part.

No script can be written until the film-maker has immersed himself thoroughly in the subject, and this means a great deal of research and, if possible, a full reconnaissance. Research not only uncovers the facts but also saves time and money in filming. The cameraman learns where best to go and at what time of the year. He also learns how to interpret behaviour: many birds, for example, give intention movements, such as a bobbing of the head, when they are about to take off, and if the cameraman knows this, he knows exactly when to start his camera for a take-off shot.

LIFE HISTORIES

The life-cycle of a particular species is one of the most difficult of all wildlife subjects to film and needs painstaking research. Where behaviour patterns are already well documented, the film-maker can usually prepare a detailed script. Inevitably, this must closely follow the events of the life-cycle in the order in which they occur, though the film may open with some sort of montage of shots from various parts of the life-cycle, or even with a short dramatic sequence taken from the middle of the story.

Usually, about half the sequences are comparatively straightforward and the other half create problems. Even with the most intensive preparations, the filming of these may well depend on a huge slice of luck, so it is as well to realize from the start that two seasons' work may be necessary on any one life-cycle. Ronald Eastman, working as a professional full-time film-maker, found that because of a run of bad luck, including film stock faults and laboratory damage, he was forced to take three seasons to complete *The Private Life of the Great Crested Grebe.*

The following is part of a life-history film script written by Jeffery Boswall for *The Private Life of the Starling*:

Sequence 4: Nest-site Selection to Incubation

Wing-waving and song of 'our' bird	COMMENTARY: By late March a starling will have selected his nest-site for the season. He defends it by song and by wing-waving. This double advertisement is usually enough. But any really persistent male contender is removed physically, by being shouldered off. Unlike many other birds the starling does not defend a tract of land, he dominates merely the nest-hole.
Collection, transportation and construction. If possible, shots of bird having difficulty with long straw, etc (interiors and exteriors)	Early in April – still unpaired – the cock starts to build the nest, and completes the main structure. It is untidy but will doubtless function quite well. The bare shell is complete

	and ready to be offered to a female.
Male giving female-attracting calls	Likely females are lured into the general area by a disyllabic 'killdeer' call or by an
Sexual chase	urgent crescendo, and then chased and driven to the nest.
Female collecting, transporting and arranging lining (exteriors and interiors)	By 9 April the birds have paired up; the female then lines the nest for herself.

ECOLOGICAL STUDIES

In the field of ecological studies, too, a lot of research must be carried out. The large number of plant and animal species involved can create a feeling of helplessness; one hardly knows where to start writing. The fact that it just is not possible to film *all* the species living in even quite a small area of woodland, marshland or heathland, must be realized and accepted; all the film can do is to give an impression of the wealth of life in these habitats.

To show the relationships and interdependence between various species, some of the food webs can be examined: for instance A is eaten by B, which in its adult form is eaten by C, which when it dies and decays provides food for D, which also provides food for B. The best way of setting about the scripting of an ecological film study is to take some of the most important of the food chains within such a web and build the film around them. If one of the members of a food chain exists in all seasons in a given habitat (a bird, for example), this may provide a lead character, or 'star', to take the film from season to season.

Ecological food webs are so complex that the choosing of only a few food chains automatically excludes a great number of species from the film story. But a cross-section of these can be introduced from time to time, some as cutaways to the main action and others during atmosphere and mood sequences. Here they may never be identified, but they will help to create the impression of great variety.

In this type of film many of the shots set out in the original script may well have to be changed, and constant revision is necessary throughout the course of filming. The purpose of the film and the structure set out in the script remain the same, but individual shots and sometimes even small sequences may be substituted when unexpected failures and successes are encountered.

The following is part of a script layout for a film study of life in an oak tree:

Action	*Notes*
Close shots and big close shots of aphids on oak leaves	Commentary establishes contact with gardeners: their bêtes-noires [the aphids]
Pans and close shots of leaves glistening with honeydew	feed on cell sap in plants and great quantities of sugar go to waste – honeydew
Variety of insects collecting honeydew	very popular with other insects
Key shots of ladybirds feeding on (a) honeydew, (b) aphids	Ladybirds are arch-enemies of aphids
Lacewings taking aphids Lacewings egg-laying	so are lacewings
Studies of lacewing eggs Lacewings hatching	Possible music cue – contrast delicacy of eggs on their tiny stalks with ravenous hunters
Larvae catching aphids or *anything*	that run amok when eggs hatch

Wood-ants climbing tree-trunk and branches	Music builds as more insects move in . . .
Big close-up of woodpecker's bill taking wood-ant, then medium shot	ends with woodpecker taking wood-ants

MOOD FILMS

An attractive little film of between five and ten minutes' duration can be made by trying to capture the atmosphere of a particular habitat at a certain season. It could be, for example, an impression of the first few hours of daylight in a deciduous wood in early spring. Such a film relies heavily on beautifully composed scenic material laced with a few good wildlife studies, though the latter are rarely developed for more than a few shots. A high standard of photography and sensitive editing are required, and often this type of film relies entirely on natural sounds, without any commentary or music at all.

The script may be no more than a few pencilled notes: ideas based on memories of certain visual effects such as the mist rising off the mirror surface of a quiet river, or dew on a spider's web. There may be a certain amount of action requiring organization – a lone fisherman, perhaps, setting off in his boat on an estuary in the early morning – but on the whole everything depends on keeping the theme in mind when filming, and waiting patiently for something to turn up in the right key. Much depends on opportunism, so a skeleton script is all that is needed:

> The river, early morning, autumn. Soft and misty, dew everywhere – on spiders' webs, on spent reed-pods from outgoing season. As sun rises, it catches the colour of red autumn leaves, river becomes blaze of colour, leaves dropping and drifting downstream . . .

EXPEDITIONS

An expedition to observe or capture a species of animal in a faraway place cannot usually be planned in any great detail in advance of the actual filming. The film has to be made as the expedition progresses, but one must remember that it is wasteful of film to shoot too much build-up material until the key shots have been secured. A certain amount of story material must be shot as it happens, simply because it will not be repeated. For example, introductory sequences of the arrival in a foreign country and a record of the journey into the interior must be filmed there and then in case they are needed. It is a gamble that has to be taken.

When shots have to be 'grabbed' in a kind of newsreel style, it is most important to have a script sesssion at the close of each day to write down exactly what has been got on film and, even more important, what has *not* been shot. For example, on one day of an animal-collecting expedition some key scenes of the capture of a particular animal may have been filmed. These consist of long shots of it being pursued and a long shot of it running into a net; then, after a break in continuity while the cameraman ran in close, there are close-ups of the animal being disentangled and examined. Without additional material this sequence would be short and in film terms almost meaningless, but by working in additional material around the existing film shots it can be made into an exciting and sustained sequence. So, later that day the cameraman makes a note of the extra shots he requires, the location is re-visited and the same operation re-enacted bit by bit: the erection of the nets, the beaters fanning out, close-ups of the beaters, reverse angle shots of people rushing up to where the animal was netted, and several cut-away shots of individual faces as the handling of the animal is mimed.

All this calls for a lot of co-operation from helpers, and the film-maker should always try to make this clear to everyone concerned before ever an expedition sets out.

12

Editing

THE general principles of editing apply just as much to wildlife films as to any other kind of film; but the wildlife cameraman is not able to exercise the same sort of control over his subject material, so the editing of his films calls for considerable ingenuity. The main difficulties at the editing stage are insufficient coverage (apparent from the lack of camera angles) coupled with lack of continuity (even when action is covered on two angles the animal concerned is often moving or facing in different directions).

WHERE TO CUT

Before deciding how to tackle these difficulties, it is worth considering the three main types of shot used in filming action, and how it is possible to cut from one shot to another.

The long shot is used to show an animal, or the interaction of several animals, at a distance, while at the same time revealing something of the immediate surroundings. It can therefore also act as an establishing shot for the sequence as a whole, and may even be useful for some violent or fast action which could not be accommodated in a closer medium shot.

The medium shot usually includes one or two animals, and may show most of the action. The close shot probably takes in only the head and shoulders of one particular animal and is useful for showing reactions, and important details such as the erection of a bird's crest feathers during courtship.

An action sequence should be covered by three types of shot, with a certain amount of overlap of action between them to allow for discretion in cutting.

A well-shot sequence can be edited in a great many different ways, so the purpose and story of a sequence must be absolutely clear in the mind of the editor. To begin with, it is best to assemble the half-dozen or so best key shots into a logical order; then the rest of the material can be examined and thought can be given as to how best this can be incorporated with the key shots.

There must be a good reason for every shot used in the sequence; because a scene is attractive to look at, it does not necessarily qualify for inclusion. Shots should be looked at over and over again until the action in them is clearly remembered, for only in this way can the best use be made of them. Then, shot by shot, they can be pieced together so that the action runs smoothly and continuously from one to another. The process is rather like putting a jigsaw puzzle together while shaping the pieces so that each fits snugly into the next.

The success of this shaping depends a great deal on the point in the action at which the film editor cuts from one shot to another. Take, for example, the sequence of a bird approaching the nest and settling on her eggs to incubate. On the editing bench, a long shot shows the complete action up to a point a few seconds after the bird has settled on the nest; in medium close shot there are the last few steps of the bird onto the nest, the bird settling, and several seconds of incubation. The easiest point at which to cut would be from a few frames after the final movement of the bird settling in long shot, to the same action point in medium shot; in fact the bird is so static in both shots that this change in angle would result in a perfectly acceptable cut. However, the cut could be greatly improved if the shots were joined *during* the action of the bird settling down on the nest. The best cutting point would be about three-quarters of the way through the bird's action, and this would mean carefully finding matching frames in the two shots.

By cutting here the film would be improved: the long shot is left as soon as it starts to get visually boring, and the viewer is watching the bird's action so intently that he will not be aware of the film cut, provided the action flows smoothly.

This example serves to illustrate a general rule: *when joining two shots of the same subject it is better to cut on action than to cut from one static position to another.* Experience helps to show at exactly which point the cut should be made, but it is usually near the beginning or end of a definite movement. Most of this movement is likely to be covered in long shot or medium shot, and only a small amount in medium or close shot. So if the action starts in close shot it is cut after just a few frames and most of the movement is taken in the wider angle shot that follows; if it starts in long shot, then only the end of it is taken in the close shot that follows. Fig 24 shows single frames from two shots of a lemur jumping. The best cut to the closer shot is just as the lemur makes contact with the tree.

When a particular animal appears in consecutive shots, it is very important that it should be facing in the same general direction in each. If, for example, it is running from left to right across the screen in long shot, then it must be moving from left to right in the close shot immediately following. However, the animal does not have to be running at exactly the same angle in respect of the camera in each shot; it could, for example, be running very nearly towards camera but slightly to the right.

If this rule of direction is not observed, there is a strong possibility that not only will there be a bad cut, which will give a visual jolt, but that the viewer will think he is looking

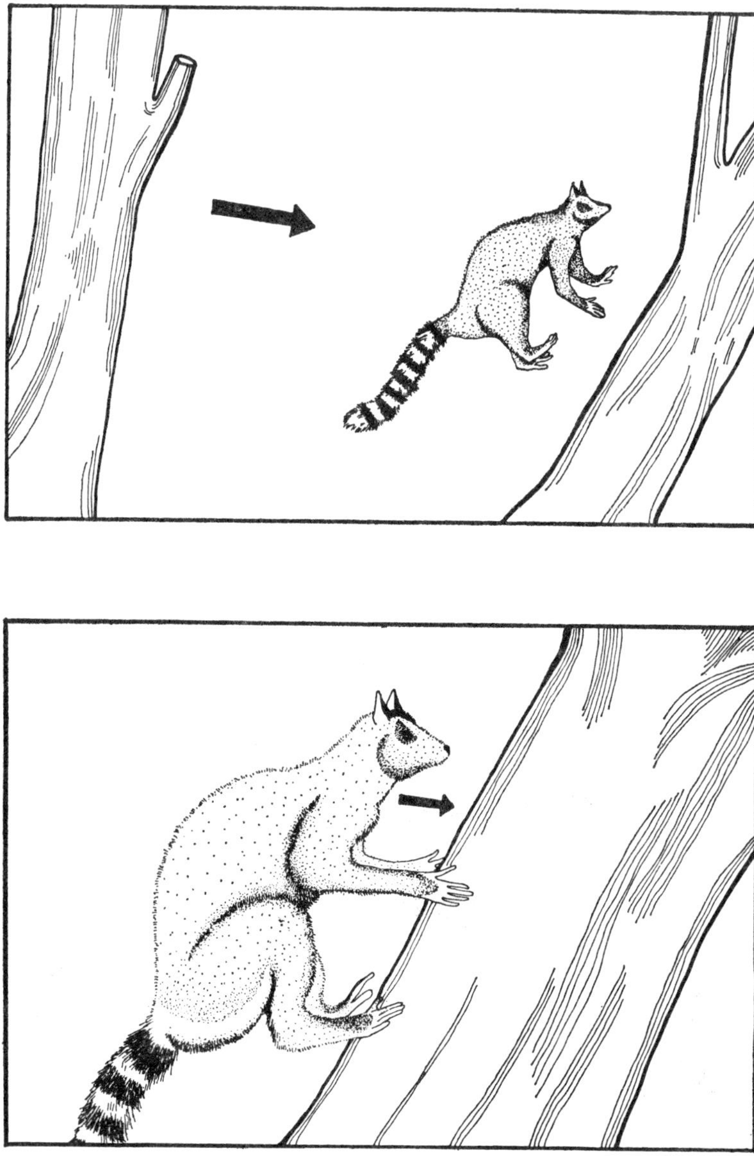

Fig 24 Cutting on action

at different animals in the two shots. If a long shot showing an animal moving left to right is followed by a medium shot of the same animal moving right to left, the viewer may well infer that the animal in the first shot is being approached by another animal moving rapidly towards it from the opposite direction.

In Fig 25 shots taken at any of the camera positions A, B and C can all be cut together, but a shot taken from position D will not intercut with any of the others.

WHAT TO DO WHEN IN DIFFICULTY

When the film coverage is adequate, it is possible to stick to these general rules, but what happens when there is little

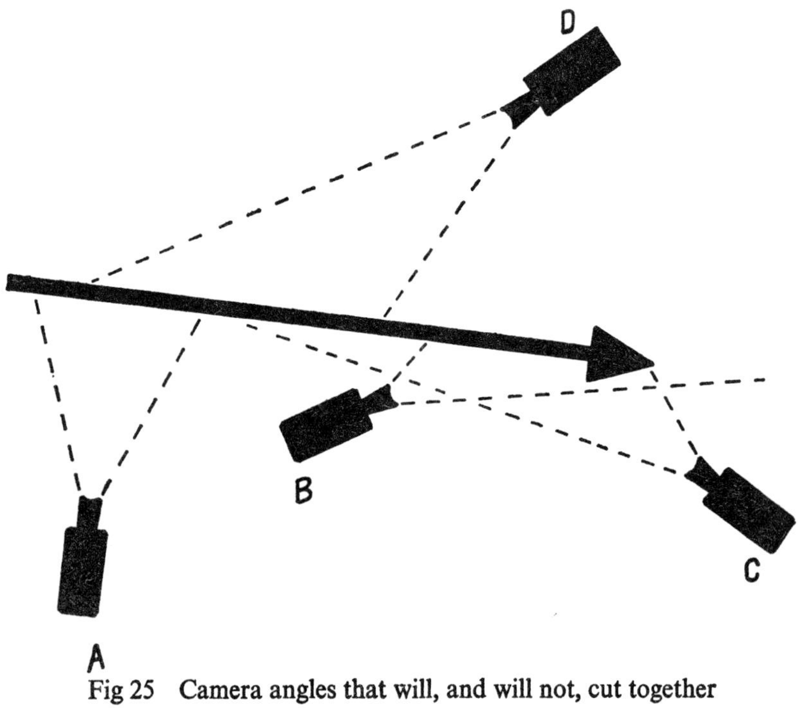

Fig 25 Camera angles that will, and will not, cut together

variety in camera angle and the direction of the action is wrong in some shots?

One solution is to put the existing film to one side and try to get better coverage later, even if it means waiting for the next season to complete the shooting. However, this may not be possible: the filming may have been done abroad and a return trip may be too costly, or the inadequate sequence may have been of a behaviour scoop that is unlikely to be seen again. If the action is almost unique, then as far as the naturalist is concerned the inadequacies of camera coverage and editing are less important. There are, however, one or two tricks that can be employed to make film look better than it really is.

In cases where all the material has been shot on one lens and there is therefore little change of angle, the joining of similar shots usually results in what is known as a jump cut. The size and position of the animal in frames of juxtaposed shots are so similar that at the film join the animal appears to make a little jump. The two shots are so alike that the animal is undoubtedly one and the same, yet for an instant the jump suggests another animal in much the same position; the viewer may also think that a few frames have been lost from the film so, all in all, there is a general reaction of bewilderment.

If the animal is static and facing in one direction, there is very little that can be done to overcome the problem. If it is moving about, however, the film editor has more of a chance. When he has to cut from one rather similar scene to another, he cuts on a matching action and this in itself helps to disguise the cut, but the quicker the action, the better this ruse will work.

Suppose that a film editor has to cut together two similar shots of a horse walking left to right, two of the horse trotting left to right, and two of the same horse galloping left to right, all taken on the same lens from the same camera angle. By matching the hoof action in the two walking shots it is possible to cut from one take to another with limited success; it is not a good cut, but at least the action is continuous. A cut between two similar trotting shots, again provided the hoof action is carefully matched, is much better, but the joining of the galloping shots is almost unnoticeable.

Sometimes a head or body turn may help to make a cut, as in two rather similar shots of a bird at its nest (Fig 26). To cut from one to the other with the bird motionless is ugly, and virtually results in a jump cut. However, if the bird makes a similar head and body movement in both shots and if the cut between the two is made during this movement, then it will be a little more acceptable. (It is assumed that both shots show important behaviour at some point; if not, the best solution is to put one of them in the dustbin.)

Insect movement is often very jerky, with sudden changes of direction occurring in a fraction of a second. The speed of this action can be seen, for example, by examining closely a film of ants. Here and there frames can be found in which the movement of an ant is just a blur because a change in direction has taken rather less than $\frac{1}{24}$ of a second. When in difficulty a film editor can take advantage of these blurred frames. It is possible to have two close shots of an ant taken with the same lens and yet avoid a jump cut, provided two such blurred frames can be found in which the movement is in the same direction, that is, clockwise or anti-clockwise. The first shot is cut immediately *after* its blurred frame, and the second cut immediately *before* its blurred frame, and the two joined together. This cut will not be noticed by most viewers, provided that the angle between the body positions in the two shots is not greater than about 120°.

DRAMATIC SITUATIONS

Every wildlife film-maker dreams of getting exciting preda-

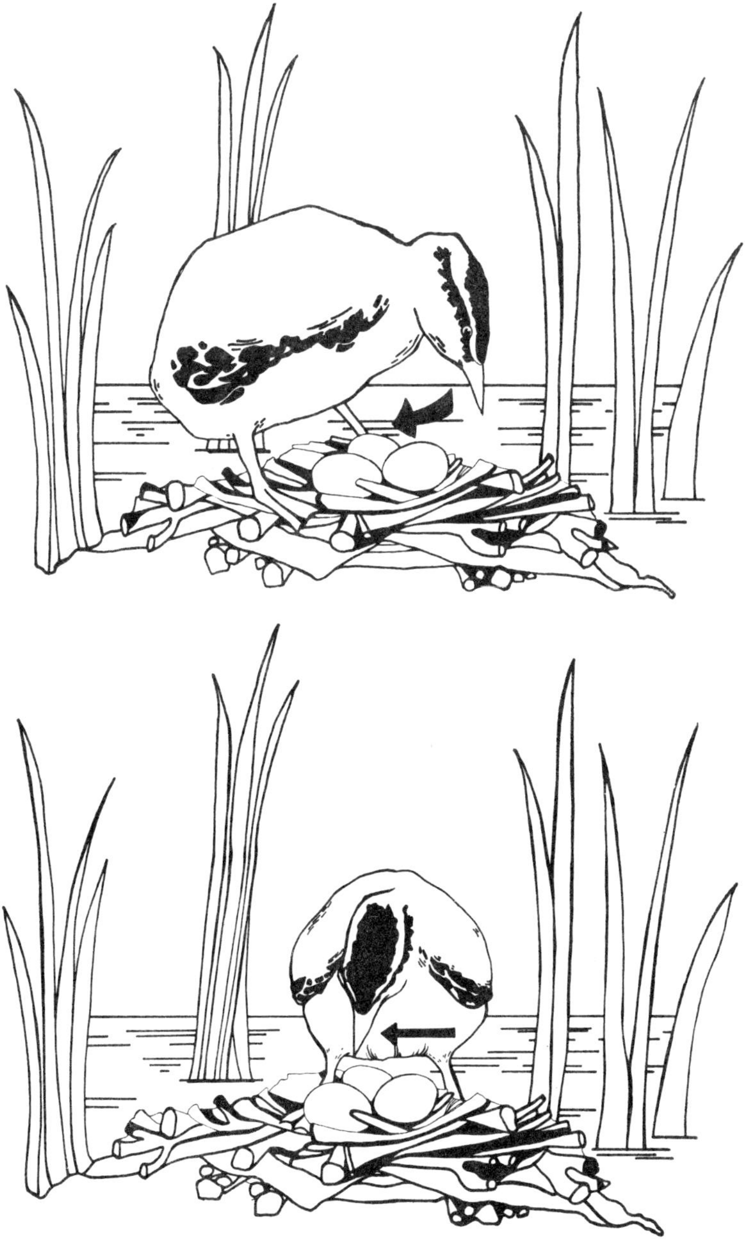

Fig 26 Making the best of a jump cut

tor/prey behaviour on film, but all too often the key shot in which the kill is made is very brief. The sequence can be built up by shooting additional scenes of both the predator and its prey (albeit with different individuals of the same species), and these can be edited together in a logical sequence immediately before the kill. In this way the audience will be prepared for what is about to happen and will be more appreciative of the action when it occurs. For example, a lucky shot of a lioness killing a zebra could be built up, first by using establishing shots of a herd of zebra grazing, a group of lions nearby, closer shots of zebra, some on the alert, a shot of a lioness stalking, zebra running away, and then the key shot of the kill. All the directions must be correct: the lioness must stalk in the same direction as she runs at the start of the kill shot, and the zebra at the alert must look in the direction of the approaching lioness; but there is no reason why a number of shots like these, taken on different occasions, should not make a perfectly acceptable, truthful, and quite dramatic sequence.

Unfortunately there are some film-makers who, when faced with a complete lack of such climactic action shots, try to make up for the deficiencies in shooting by contrived editing. It is true that a film can be made or ruined in the editing, but the behaviour of an animal cannot simply be concocted if the key section of a sequence has not been filmed in the first place. Intercutting between prey and predator with shots taken on different occasions simply does not add up to drama if no drama ever actually occurred. For example, a series of shots of a bird of prey could be intercut with a corresponding series of close-ups of a vole, and a feeling of expectation be built up in the audience. But if no action results and the two do not even appear in the same shot at any point, the audience is disappointed and feels cheated.

Page 173

(*right*) A fish-eye view of the surface. This glass-bottomed dish was used to obtain a fish's view of a mayfly on the surface of a river; (*below*) getting new and exciting camera angles. Here Ronald Eastman has enclosed the camera in a home-made watertight blimp in order to get a trout's-eye view at the end of an angler's line. The battery pack for the electrically-driven camera is slung from his neck to keep it dry.

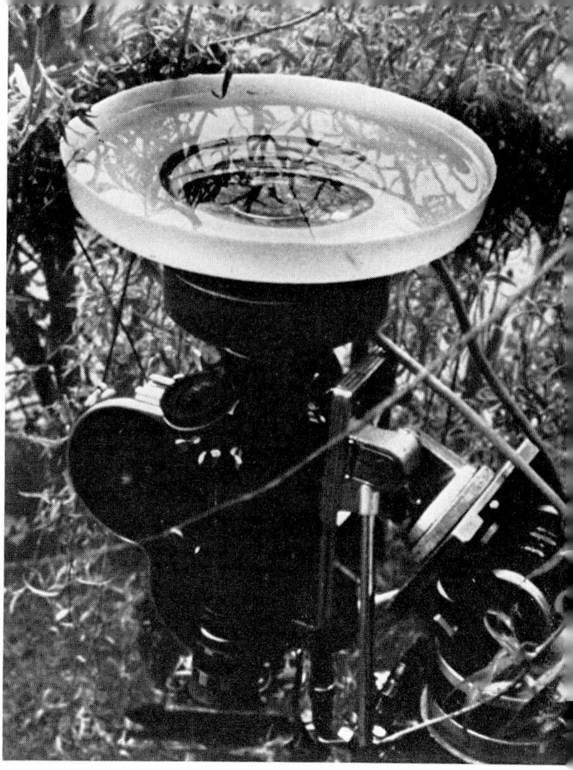

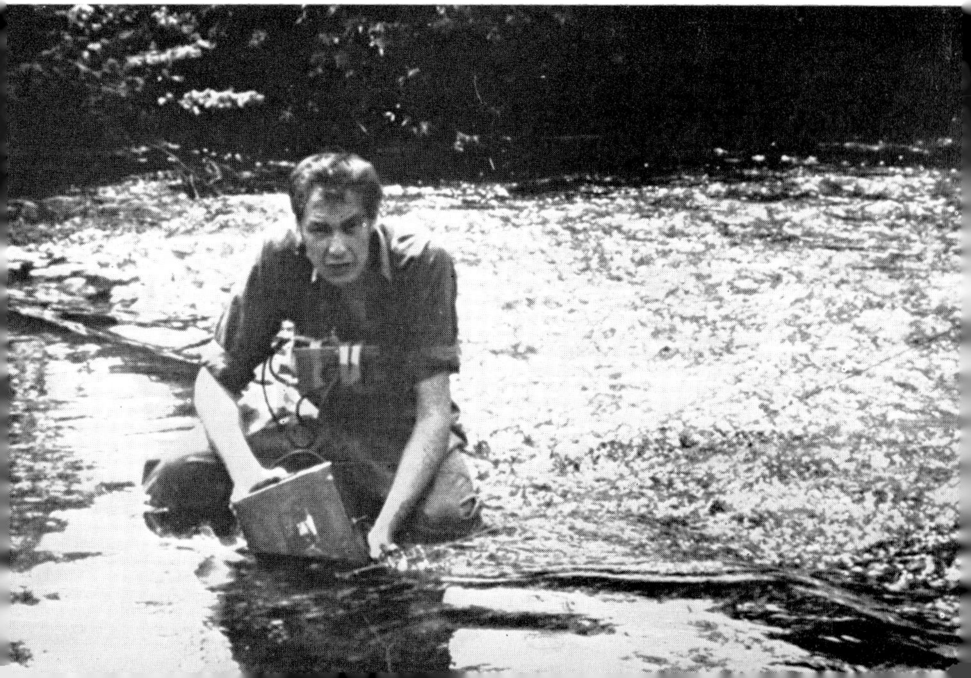

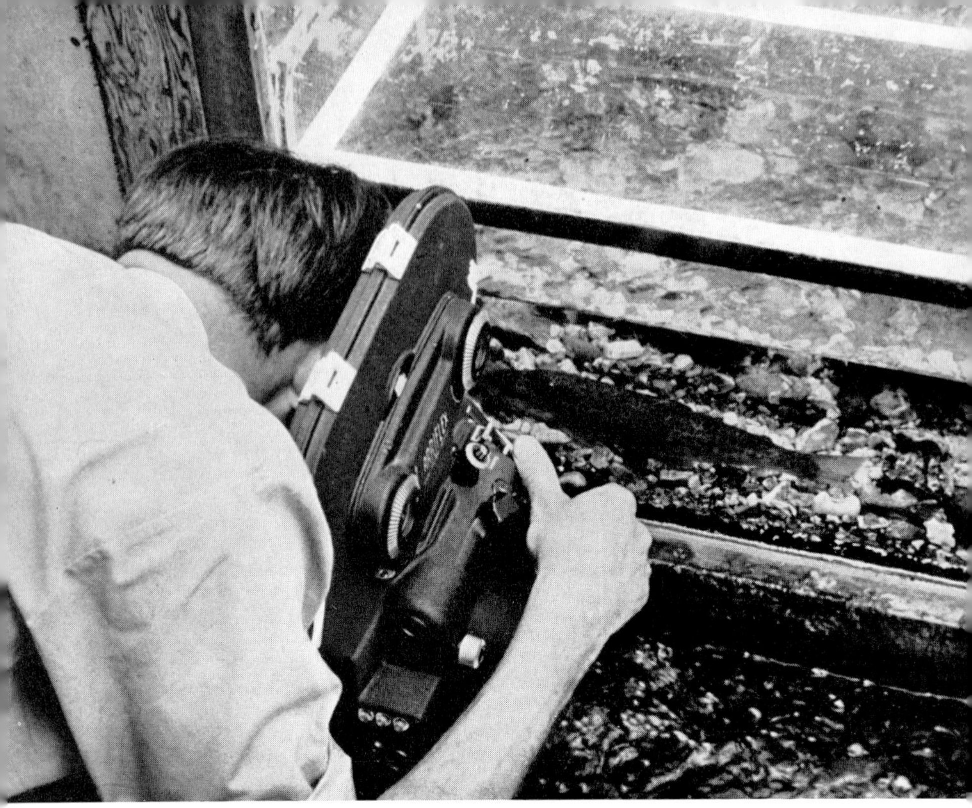

Page 174 An aquarium in a river: filming trout in a construction similar to that shown in Fig 14.

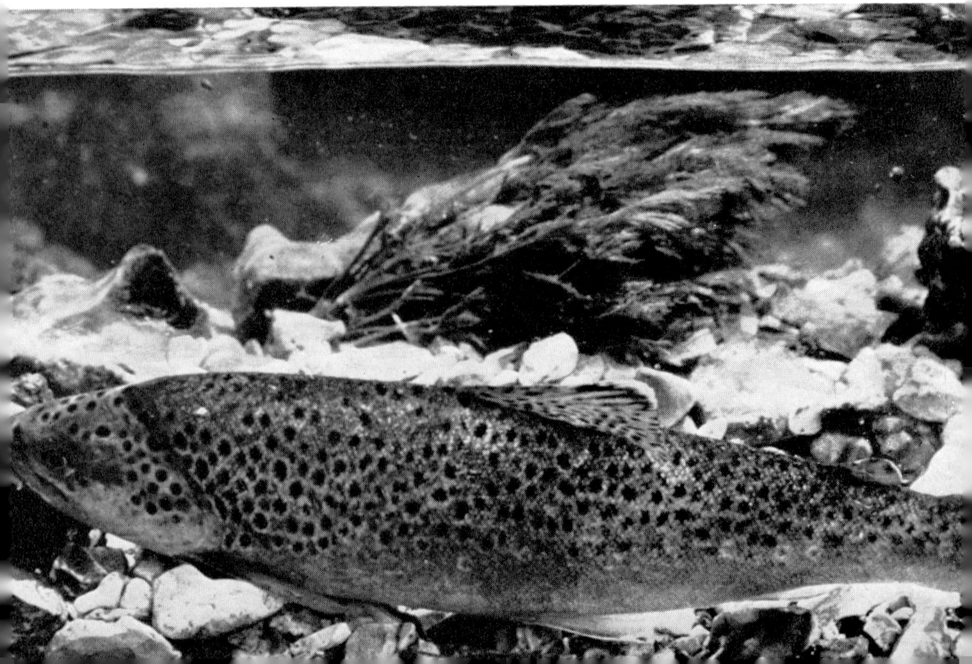

LENGTH OF SHOTS

In most wildlife films the actual length of each animal shot is dictated mainly by the action that it shows, and by the points at which it is necessary to join it for reasons of continuity to the shots on either side. Where there is a considerable range of choice, the length is also determined by the visual interest within the scene and by the rhythm and pace required during that particular sequence.

When a complete action takes place in one film shot and there are no dull moments in it, then it is best to leave it alone and let it run its full length. If there is a six-second hang-up in the middle and it is felt that this spoils the rhythm of the sequence, then a cut and the insertion of another relevant shot will keep everything moving. In dramatic action sequences, the general rule is for the first establishing shots to be rather long in running time; then, as the action begins, one should increase the speed of cutting, that is, the rate of changing from one shot to the next. At the same time the size of the shot should also increase, so that in a predator/prey sequence the penultimate shot to the kill is a one-second or two-second close-up of the quarry panicking.

In 'mood' and non-action sequences (consisting of various establishing scenes), the beginner may find it a little harder to judge the length of shots. Generally speaking, quiet lazy moods are evoked by slowish pans and static shots held for longer than usual. The atmosphere of a quiet estuary at dawn on a completely windless and slightly misty morning would be completely destroyed by five or six shots each cut to three seconds in length, even if each scene captured the required mood pictorially. The desired effect is more likely to be created by shots lasting some six or seven seconds (but not necessarily all the same length), and some distant action: a long shot of a solitary oystercatcher probing on a mudbank might be appropriate, but a close-up of dunlin busily feeding would not.

CUTTING RATIOS

A well-edited film from which all sub-standard shots have been ruthlessly omitted inevitably means that the proportion of film used in relation to film shot is small; footage lost in overlapping action and in obtaining the required rhythms will see to that. Therefore it is unlikely that any wildlife film will run to more than a third or a quarter of the original exposed footage.

For anyone working solely on an amateur basis this is hard to accept; film is by no means cheap, and a lot of time and effort has gone into filming all those discarded shots. However, this is a general condition of film-making, and it is as well for the amateur cameraman to keep in mind from the beginning that a shooting ration of 3 : 1 is good. There may be rare occasions when things can be so well planned and filming accomplished with so few hitches that a 2 : 1 ratio is achieved, but few professional wildlife films have better ratios than 4: 1, and the average figure for most television natural history films is 8 : 1.

13

Sound

THERE are three elements in a film sound track: effects, music and speech (which is usually in the form of a commentary). Many amateur cameramen with modest equipment may have previously found it economically impossible even to consider adding a sound track to their films. However, with the advent of stripe on 8mm film, and of projectors that enable synchronization to be made with a tape recorder, a new dimension is being added to many home movies.

Although most of a sound track may have to be made when the visual part of the film is complete, considerable thought should be given to it during the actual filming. Not only is it more efficient to record sound at about the same time as a sequence is shot (if you miss it then, you may have to wait until next year), but sounds that have a special part to play in the film may also have some bearing on choice of pictures and length of shots.

One way of introducing a particular animal is to use its call out of vision; this sometimes gives a more dramatic opening to a sequence than a shot of the animal itself. A sequence of the rut of red deer, for example, could start with 'atmospheric' forest scenes in early morning mist, not a single deer in sight, but in the distance the sound of the stag bellowing.

THE RECORDING OF EFFECTS

Natural sound is usually the most important of the three elements of sound track in wildlife films. A woodland sequence with a bird-song tape running behind it will have an extra dimension. This is as far as many amateurs will go, for they prefer to add any necessary commentary in person when showing their films at home or at a public lecture.

A natural sound track has two categories of sound: (a) those providing the general atmosphere and consisting of distant bird-song and other animal noises, together with any pertinent man-made noises; (b) specific noises at a higher level – a dog barking, a gate closing, a bird singing, a tern diving – all relating to action on the screen. These usually present difficulties for the amateur, since post-synchronization of them involves sophisticated and expensive equipment (more will be said about this in the next chapter). Therefore it is usually better to concentrate on the use of background atmosphere tapes.

The recording of an atmosphere tape might seem, on the face of it, to be one of the simplest of all tasks. A microphone, a good quality tape recorder (preferably one that runs at $7\frac{1}{2}$ ips), and a pair of headphones to monitor what is being recorded, are all that is needed. Once in the field, however, with the microphone placed in a suitable position, the recordist has only to don the headphones to realize the problems he is up against.

The first trouble comes with weather. A loud rumbling is heard which seems to bear no relation to the breeze that up till then was scarcely noticeable. If the wind is really very slight, a wind shield can be placed on the microphone, but if it is at all gusty and the microphone cannot be sheltered even by repositioning it, then recording will have to be abandoned.

The day eventually arrives when there appears to be a dead

calm. The recorder is set up and started, and almost immediately the distant droning of an approaching aircraft is heard; it takes two minutes to arrive and twice as long to disappear. Then comes the realization that because the air is so still all the sounds from a distant main road are being clearly picked up by the microphone. The microphone is realigned to make these less noticeable. Thirty seconds later, a tractor starts working in the adjoining field. There is nothing for it but to wait until the driver has his mid-morning break, or abandon the attempt yet again, or move elsewhere. And so it goes on, until finally the time comes when everything appears to be going right. Then and only then, as he listens to the sounds being recorded, is the recordist aware of a very dominant call repeated over and over again very close to the microphone. It is the alarm call of a blue tit, perturbed by human interference near its nest or by the microphone with its long silver snake-like lead glinting in the sun.

Such a series of incidents is by no means unusual. The recording of natural sound is not a job that can be rushed. In order to avoid alarming blue tits and other birds, it may be necessary to record from a hide, or at least to make sure that the microphone and lead are well camouflaged. This is especially important when the microphone is tied to the branch of a tree near a birds' perching place. Sometimes it is convenient to have a tape recorder in the hide at the same time as the film is being shot; the microphone and lead can be laid out and camouflaged in advance. There may be occasions when the cameraman is waiting for light, or for the subject to return, when he can usefully make sound recordings instead.

When conditions are suitable for an atmosphere recording, it should be made at the highest level possible without risk of distortion. If the microphone has been placed wisely there will be a blend of distant effects and bird and animal calls, not one of which will drown the others, and no disturbing foreground noise. The reason for recording this mixture at as high a level as possible is that it may subsequently have to be re-recorded when the final sound track is made, and further amplification may increase unwanted tape noise.

Another point worth remembering is that it is advisable to record much more sound than is actually required. This will give the editor freedom to select when he listens to the recording, perhaps more critically, at a later date.

Some of the problems involved in getting a good recording of a specific bird or animal can be lessened by the use of a parabolic reflector. With this, the microphone is fixed close to the focus of the paraboloid so that sound waves striking the concave surface of the reflector are concentrated at the microphone. The reflector, which may be anything from eighteen inches to four feet in diameter, is placed on the ground or on a tripod (or even held in the hand), and directed at the subject, which may be fifty feet or even more away. The reflector concentrates sound coming from a comparatively narrow angle (Fig 27), so unwanted noises and calls of other animals outside this angle of acceptance are kept well in the background. However, *all* sounds behind and in line with the subject and the reflector are also greatly amplified, and the unwanted noise of a chain saw or passing train could have a more disastrous effect than ever on the recording.

The parabolic reflector is most useful for recording single species. It can also be used for making atmosphere recordings, by taking a 'slice' of sound from a particular habitat. Here the method is to set up the reflector and microphone and move it around a few degrees at a time until a satisfactory blend of animal voices is found, without any one species obliterating the others.

SYNCHRONIZATION OF SOUND AND PICTURE

Even professional wildlife film-makers rarely film animal action and sound at one and the same time by using synchro-

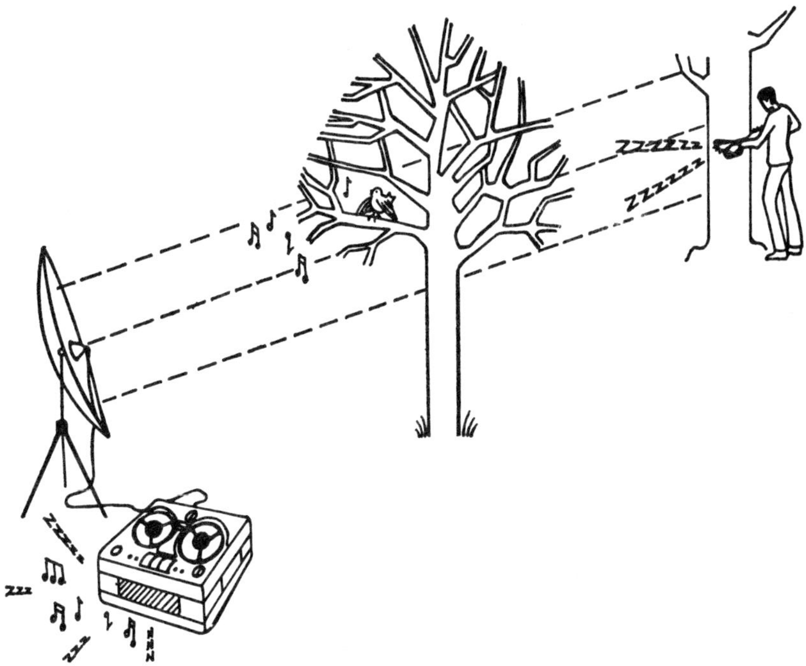

Fig 27 A parabolic reflector collects *all* sounds that are in line with it

nized equipment: it involves much more elaborate and heavier apparatus, and optimum conditions occur very infrequently. The usual system of synchronization is for the camera to be linked electrically to the tape recorder, so that a guide pulse is recorded onto one half of the tape and the actual recording onto the other. The tape is transferred afterwards to sprocketed magnetically-coated film at a recording studio, and the pulse ensures that synchronization is maintained throughout this operation. Sound and picture are then edited on two separate films (double headed) on an editing machine.

The amateur cannot afford such a highly sophisticated process, but some of the cameras available now allow him to record sound directly onto a stripe on the side of the exposed film. A separate tape recorder is not required, and synchronization is automatic. But the camera must be effectively blimped or, alternatively, the microphone must be placed very close to the subject and at such a distance from the camera that its mechanical sound is not picked up. Ideally, a parabolic reflector should be used.

One of the few pieces of wildlife behaviour really worth trying to film by using synchronization in the field is that of birds singing. But though the whereabouts of song perches may be known, it may be days before conditions are satisfactory for both sound and camera. This probably explains why so little of this type of work has been done, except with birds in captivity.

MAKING AN EFFECTS SOUND TRACK

In its simplest form, an effects sound track in a wildlife film consists of continuous background atmosphere appropriate to the scene on the screen. For example, a short five-minute film set entirely in one small wood in the early morning could be effectively supported by one good atmosphere tape running continuously throughout the film. Here the sound can be played directly from a tape recorder, and there is no need to use a film stripe.

When the film consists of a number of sequences shot in several locations at different times of the year, many different recordings have to be used and re-recorded onto the film stripe, or onto another tape which can be run in synchronization with the projector.

The re-recording process necessary to make the film sound track involves the use of at least two tape recorders and a mixing unit. For a film using atmosphere tapes only, the method is as follows. First the edited film is run through and each sequence that needs a different type of sound backing is timed. Armed with the details of the required lengths of each separate band of atmosphere, the next stage is to listen carefully to each available tape and choose the best relevant sections. For example, there may be an estuary sequence opening with two establishing shots of twelve seconds' duration, in which all the birds are very distant, after which a number of waders are seen closer to the camera. By carefully listening to the tape, it should be possible to find a suitable section of the required length in which there are no close calls and which would match the opening of this film sequence. The section is then copied, or edited out, allowing about ten seconds overlength, five seconds extra at the beginning and five at the end.

This process is repeated for each new film sequence, and all the separate tapes are then joined up in two reels. On reel 1 are joined the tracks for sequences 1, 3, 5, 7 and so on, and on reel 2 the tracks for sequences 2, 4, 6 etc. Each band of atmosphere is joined to the next by a short section of coloured leader tape so that the beginning and end of each sound recording can be readily and visually found.

At this point some preparations have usually to be made on the film. During recording, a knowledge is required of exactly when a sequence ends and another begins, not only a fraction of a second before it actually happens, but two or three seconds before that as well. So small pieces of thin opaque tape (Fig 28) are stuck to the celluloid base over the picture area, at a point about ten frames before a sequence ends and a new one begins, and at another point about fifty frames before this change. This applies to projection at 16 or 18fps; at 24fps, 15 and 75 frames respectively are appropriate positions.

Preparations are now nearly complete for re-recording the two prepared tapes onto the film stripe, but first a simple chart must be made, for the next operation needs a very clear head, and two helpers if possible. The chart should

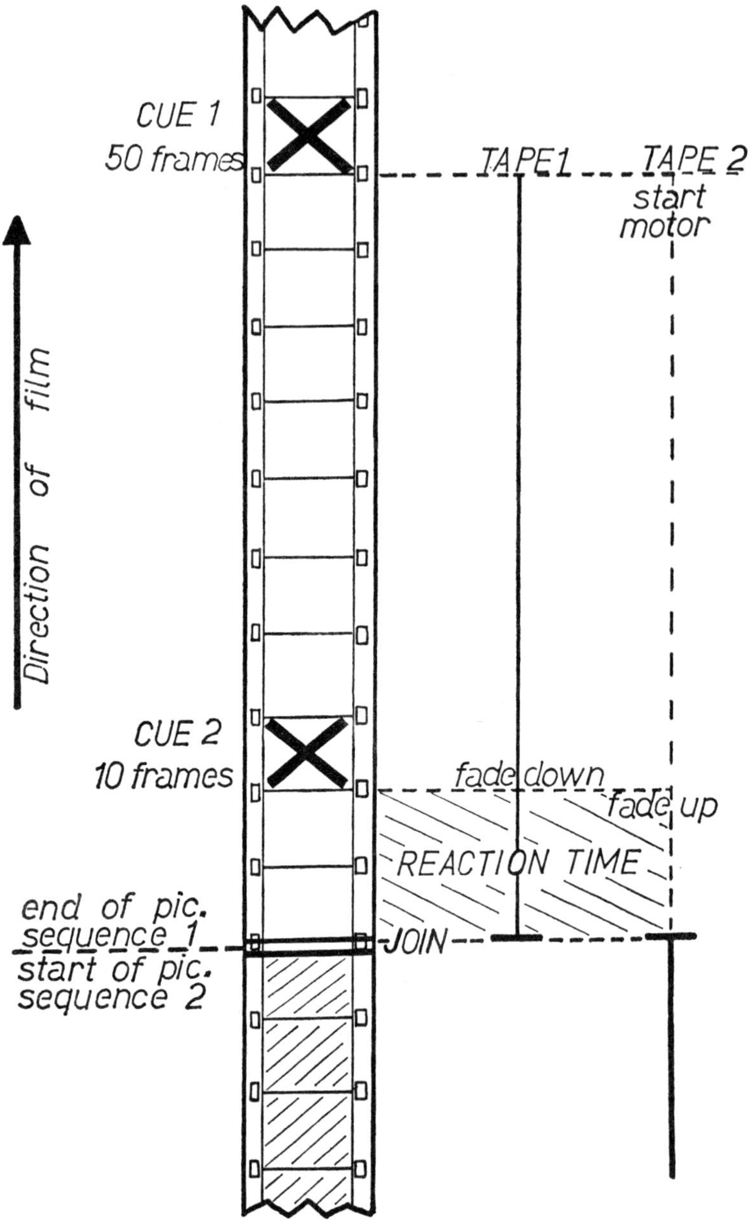

Fig 28 Marking film for simple atmosphere sound track

show the approximate points at which the various tracks begin and end, the exact positions being cued by the tabs that have been stuck onto the film.

The timings are measured from the start of the film, and the first track on tape 1 is begun a few seconds before the first frame of picture appears, so that it can be faded up at zero. Look at the chart in Fig 29. As sequence 1B approaches, tape 2 machine is started on the first visual cue. As sequence 1B begins, the level of effects on tape 1 machine is reduced and tape 2 machine is faded in at low level. Then the two Vs on the chart indicate a slow mixing of sounds, so that tape 1 machine has been completely faded out by the start of

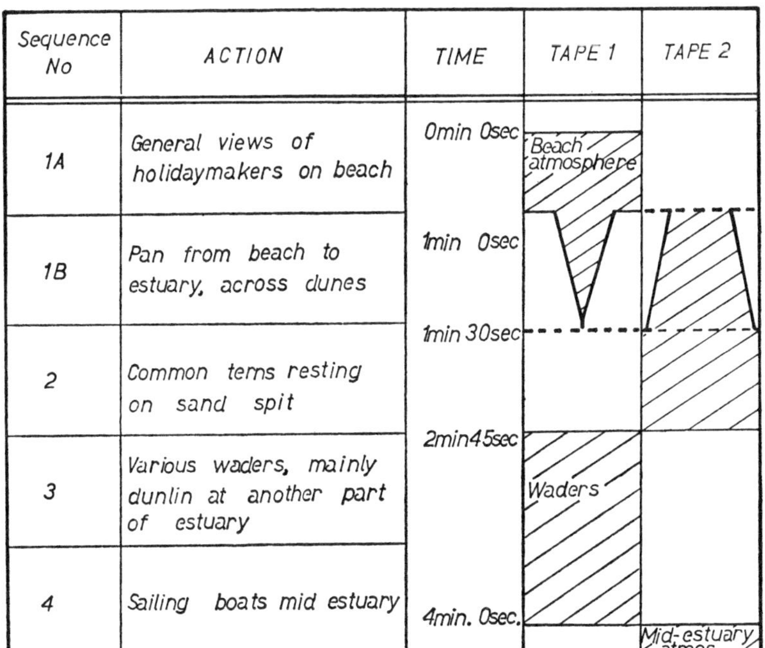

Fig 29 Guide chart for recording atmosphere sound track

sequence 2, and at this point tape machine 2 only is being used. By now tape 1 machine will have run onto coloured leader tape, where it can be stopped until just before sequence 3 is reached. The transition from sequence 1 to 2 through 1B is a slow sound mix, but between 3 and 4 it is virtually a sound cut, achieved by flipping the faders on the mixer unit as fast as possible.

This is a simple application of methods used in professional film recording, where most of the sound sources would be magnetic film tracks locked electronically to the action film. In amateur circles ingenuity has to be used to adapt any available equipment for this purpose. Fortunately more and more modern projectors have devices that aid simple sound-track construction.

COMMENTARY

Recording commentary onto striped film is quite simple when no other sources of sound are used. At home, the main difficulty lies in screening the microphone from projector noise so that this is not picked up with the commentator's voice. If the projector is rested on a soft surface, there should be no amplification of mechanical noise. The picture can be back-projected, or projected via a mirror, so that the live side of the speaker's microphone is not in line with the projector. The speaker himself can also be screened, to reduce projector noise even further and also to avoid any boxed or echoey acoustic effect.

The complicated procedure for the making of a mixed sound track of effects and commentary lies beyond the scope of most amateurs, though the usual method is an extension of the process already described for mixing two effects tapes. It is worth noting, however, that new equipment is being introduced which makes the process easier; already there are projectors on the market enabling commentary to be recorded over an existing music or effects track that automatically drops in level when speech is added.

The question of when to talk and when not to is important. The term 'commentary' is unfortunate because it suggests the non-stop description of a football match or a ceremonial occasion by a radio commentator. Nothing could be less desirable in a film than a continuous accompaniment of words; if this is really necessary to make the audience understand what is going on, then the film is a failure.

If sound is used at all, then the commentary should be considered as just one strand of information, and a secondary strand at that. The pictures should tell most of the story, and words should only be used to convey information that cannot be shown visually. The action should not be described in the commentary since this simply duplicates information, but supplementary details and interpretation of behaviour are valuable and give the audience a greater understanding of the action.

In the course of watching a film, the viewer's concentration is bound to fluctuate. On action sequences his attention is so taken up by the pictures that commentary is a waste of time. Sometimes a few words of explanation are necessary, but they should be as succinct as possible and dovetailed into short lulls in the action. Longer sections of commentary usually go with slower sequences of film, best of all with introductory long shots and establishing scenes. By careful placing of words in this way, with frequent rests from the commentator's voice, the interest of the audience can be maintained in the less visually attractive sequences. This is well demonstrated in the prize-winning film *Signals for Survival* (see page 63); the skill of Hugh Falkus's commentary can be appreciated even in the following short extract from the filmscript. (Shots are given in abbreviated form.)

Vision	*Sound*
MS Pair of gulls at nest-site	On many occasions the male has already been taking the female house-hunting, to
MCS Gull at nest-site	interest her in a possible nest-site.
CU Gull calling	(Male gull 'mewing')
MLS Pair of gulls at nest-site	He mews. The female joins him. And in gull language they tell each other that 'this
MS ditto, 'choking'	is the place to build'.
MS Pair of sitting gulls choking	This display is called 'choking', and the birds will do it time after time.
MS Pair at nest-site choking	(Pair of gulls choking)
	That both partners should agree on the position of the nest is essential, because they take it in turns to incubate the eggs.
MCS Gull choking	The repetition of choking helps to imprint the memory
MS Pair at nest-site choking	of the nest-site. They *must* agree that 'this is the place'.
	(Pair of gulls choking)
MLS Two pairs facing each other across boundary, with male herring gull in background	The female has to learn the boundaries of her mate's territory. She does this by watching his disputes with the birds next door. That male herring gull in the background is *not* one of a mixed

	pair. He's just a bystander, guarding his own territorial boundary.
MLS Two females fighting with male looking on	(General colony noises, wing flaps and scuffles)
	The female may join in these boundary disputes herself, and when she does she usually goes for the other female.
	(General colony noises, wing flaps and scuffles)
MLS Pair running R to L choking	After an argument with their neighbours, a pair will run off and have a good choke together on the nest-site.
	(Pair of gulls choking)
MS Pair settling and choking DISSOLVE TO: MS Pair at nest-site	This serves a double purpose. It tells their neighbours to keep off, and also helps to cement their own friendship. Their boundaries have been threatened. They have fought the enemy in a common cause. Now they are at peace, together.

MUSIC

The thought of a single note of music being part of the sound track of a wildlife film makes some people shudder. I myself am convinced that music is an important and emotive element in film-making, but I am prepared to admit that it is frequently misused. The commonest fault is to smother the entire film in musical wallpaper. In a lot of films a light orchestra plays gay tunes non-stop behind commentary, and is heard at full level in the breaks between commentary. Second-rate documentary film-makers no doubt hope that this sort of musical accompaniment will lull the audience into a benign acceptance of the shortcomings of the film.

Music in films should never be an accompaniment but an integral part, one strand of a complex weave of pictures, effects, words and music. This is why the mere adding of previously recorded music to an edited film is seldom very successful. There are only two ways to achieve integration of music and action. The first is to edit the picture, then write and record music specially to match. The second is to find a piece of music that more or less matches the cut action of the film, then fine-cut the picture to match the rhythms of the music. The title sequences at the beginning and end of a film can sometimes be treated differently. If the music is to be restricted to these, it is usually possible to choose suitable short sections and add them straight from the disc without too much difficulty.

Music should be used sparingly in any documentary film, but even more carefully in wildlife films; in strictly scientific behaviour films it is out of place in any case. Remember that there is usually a wide range of natural music available; the voices of birds and animals can often be used not only for their aesthetic effect, but sometimes quite dramatically. In some wildlife films, however, it is not possible to make much use of natural sound, in insect studies for example, and if the film-maker feels that the use of music is justified then there is no reason why he should deprive himself of one of the most valuable tools of his trade.

Apart from title sequences, music is most likely to be useful for mood sequences or with montages of shots of expedition activities. The transition from one season to another, for

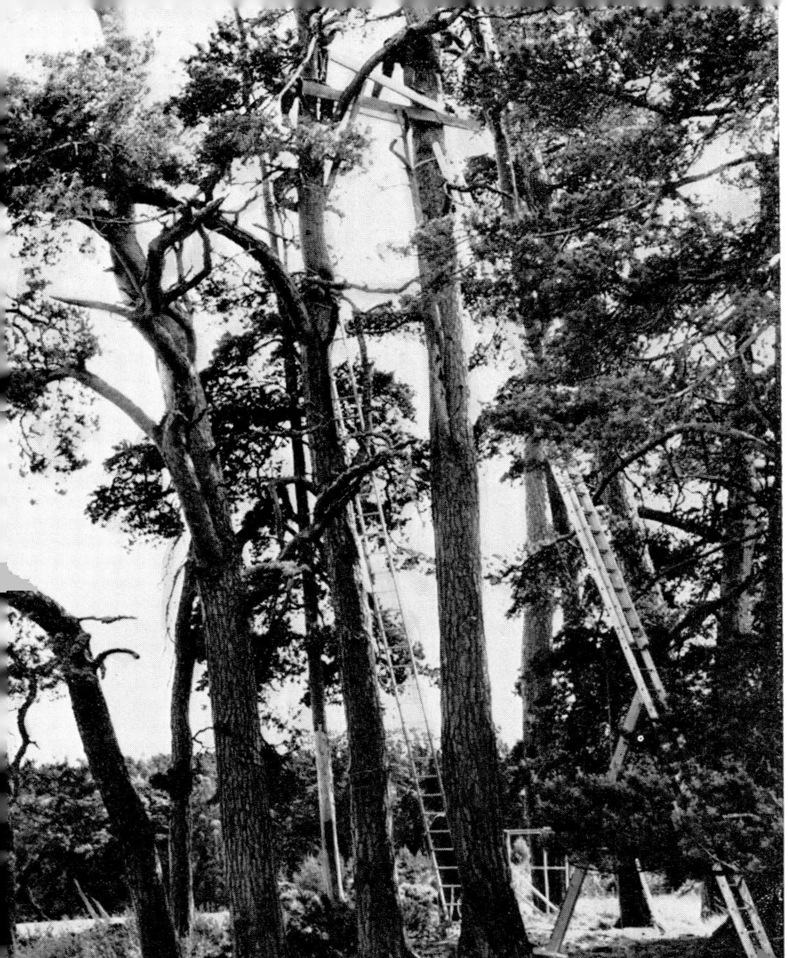

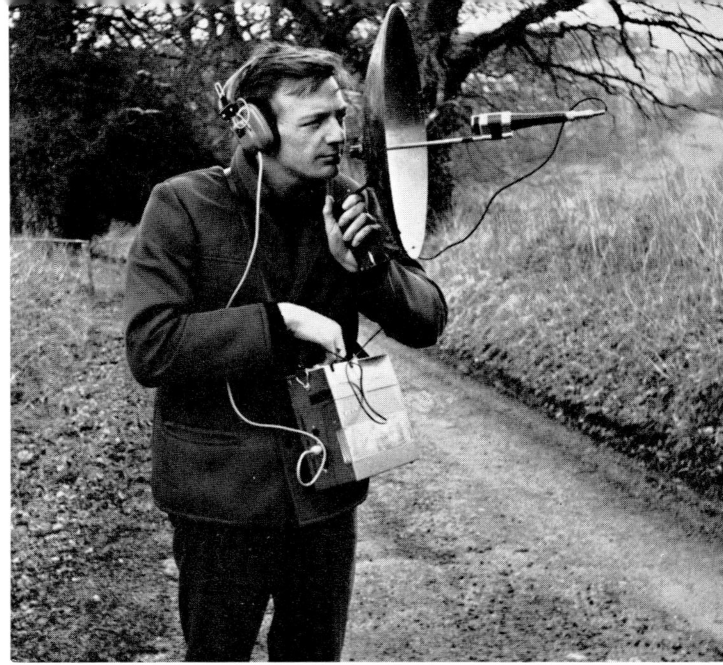

Page 191

(*left*) Constructing a hide platform by bracing three trees together with planks. This was built for filming ospreys at a secret site in 1967, and it was just as important for the hide to be concealed from the public as it was for the birds not to be disturbed. Nest shots were taken at a distance of 60yd with a 600mm Kilfitt lens; (*above*) the use of a parabolic reflector to 'focus' the microphone, and exclude unwanted sounds. Larger versions may be mounted on a tripod.

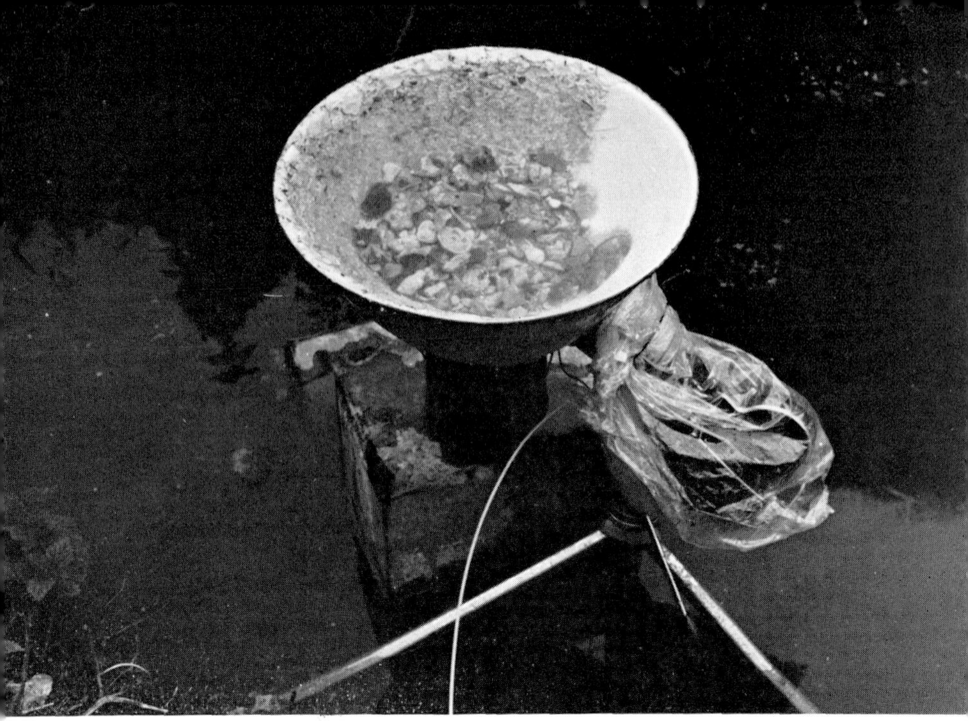

Page 192 How to film a kingfisher feeding under water: (*above*) the camera, which is wrapped in polythene to keep it dry, is fixed in such a position that it looks through a small window inset in the bottom of a bowl. A wide-angled lens is used to take in part of the bottom of the bowl, which is covered in small stones to stimulate the stream bed. The camera is operated remotely from a hide nearby; (*below*) the position of the filming bowl and camera in the stream, with the hide on the bank.

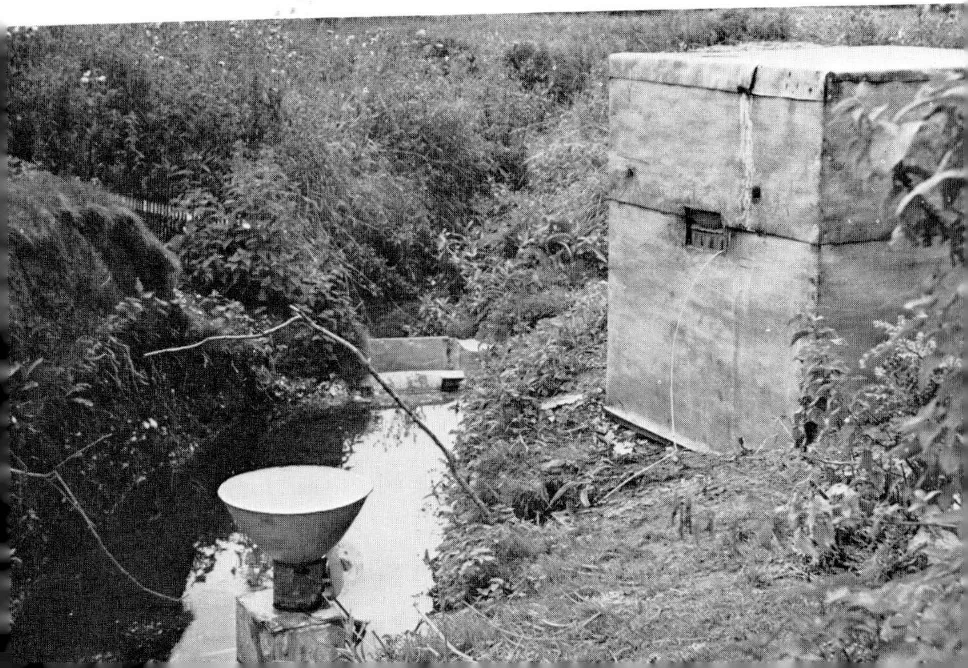

example, can be effected by mood-setting music; and the loneliness of a desert, the starkness of marshy salines, the grandeur of a rocky mountainous scene, may all be emphasized more dramatically with music than with words.

There are strict regulations about the use of commercial records in film sound tracks, and the company concerned should always be consulted. Several companies, however, have extensive libraries of music recorded specially for use in films and in television. Most of it consists of nondescript cheerful tunes, sports marches, and short atmospheric passages such as are used for newsreels and cheap magazine-type documentaries, but it is sometimes possible to find among all this some quite distinctive and well-written music.

When choosing music for a film, it is better to be consistent and use the same type of orchestra and the same style throughout, even though the moods of various passages may vary. This gives the film cohesion, and if the music has come from several different sources the viewer will be less aware of this fact. Ideally, the music should come from one work, even if only comparatively short sections are used. In this way all the musical sequences are related and it may even be possible to arrange the selected passages so that a certain theme reappears in several different moods.

Whenever possible, avoid fading in or out in mid-phrase. This always sounds untidy and gives the impression that the music does not belong to the film. If a piece of music is really difficult to fade out because it lacks phrases that have a definite end, then it should be dipped behind commentary or important effects before fading out.

There are occasions, though they should be few and far between, when a commentary line has to be spoken during a music sequence. Within the limits set by the relevance of the words to the pictures, the timing of such a line in respect of the musical phrasing is important. If the length of a complete phrase in the music is not the same as the length of a section of commentary, do not arrange to fade up the music in the middle of a phrase. Try instead to advance the commentary section. It is always better to fade down music in mid-phrase at the start of a commentary line, so that it can be faded up again at the start of the next phrase.

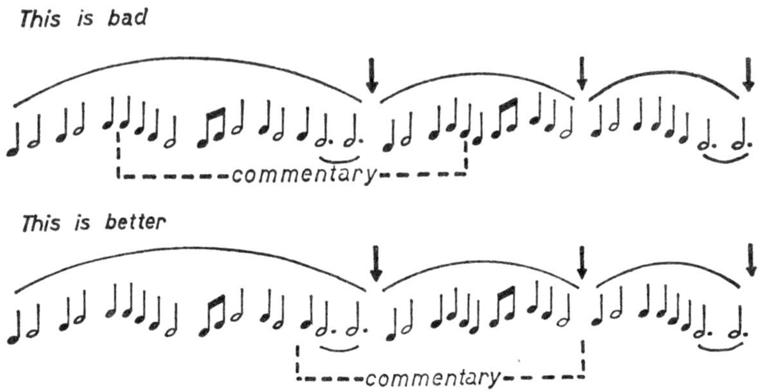

Fig 30 Phrasing music and commentary in a sound track

Specially written music is usually beyond the reach of most amateurs and even of professionals with modest budgets, but for those who can afford it there is great satisfaction to be found in having music composed to suit the exact requirements of the film. Fortunately most wildlife subjects are best served by small groups of instruments, or even solo instruments. The piano and the organ are rarely suitable, but classical guitar and harp have been used to good effect on many occasions, and the accordion or harmonica give a salty flavour to films about the coastline or the sea.

14

Club and Society Films

THERE are hundreds of natural history societies, each one, no doubt, with a sprinkling of cine enthusiasts among its members. Quite often such a society wishes to produce a film, perhaps just for pleasure or perhaps to draw public attention to some aspect of conservation in their area. There are many advantages in a combined film effort, and also several pitfalls. It is as well to consider these carefully before embarking on an ambitious project, so that precious time and money will not be wasted.

First of all it is necessary to appoint a director. Several different cameramen, each with their own special tasks, can contribute to a film, but it is fatal to have more than one director. So before starting the film, the group should elect one person to supervise the whole work, preferably someone whose knowledge and experience of film-making is respected. After that, individuals should feed the director with ideas, but if he chooses not to use them they must swallow their pride and get on with their own appointed jobs.

AVOIDING THE PITFALLS

All cameras used in a club project should be correctly aligned, so that the frame line, that is the division between consecutive frames of cine film, coincides with the mid-point of the sprocket hole (Fig 31a). In a film taken on one camera only, incorrect alignment (Fig 31b) is no great problem; the projector has to be racked slightly up or down at the start and all is well. If, however, a film is made up of various shots taken with a variety of cameras, some correctly aligned and others not, then it will need continuous and irritating adjustment throughout projection. This can be avoided by checking alignments before filming starts and, if necessary, returning faulty cameras to the makers or the main dealers for servicing.

Uniformity of camera speed may seem an elementary point, but unless it is mentioned it is possible that some cameramen in the group will shoot at 16 or 18fps, while the others go ahead at 24fps. If the intention is to put sound on stripe using amateur equipment, the slower speeds will do,

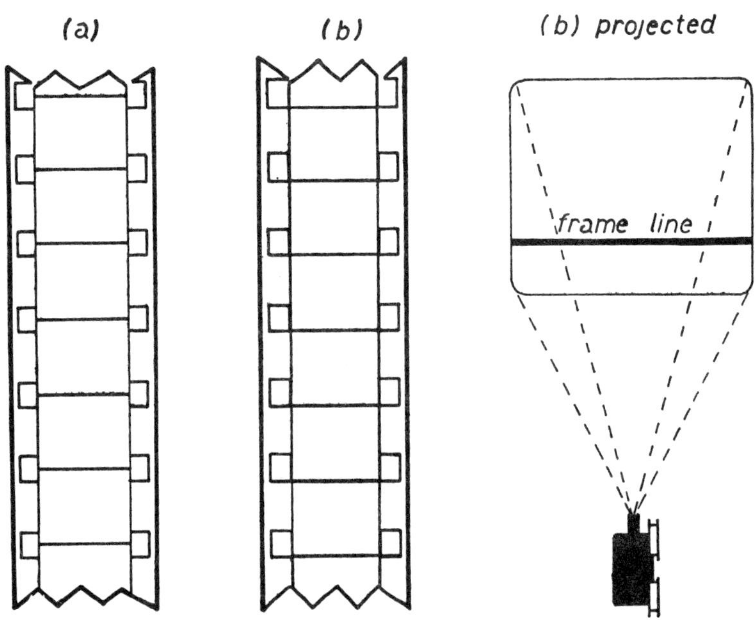

Fig 31 Discrepancy in frame lines on different cameras

provided they are used by all cameramen, but if professional equipment is to be hired to complete the sound track, then 24fps is the speed to use.

Right from the start everyone must agree to shoot on the same film stock or the same stock range. If some outstanding sequences already exist and are unlikely to be repeatable, then these may determine the choice of stock for the rest of the production, but unless it is almost unique existing film may have to be written off.

If the film is to be shown many times and several copies are needed, then on 16mm the choice lies between the Ektachrome range or Eastmancolor. The former are reversal films, the latter a negative/positive process; but in each case the original which passes through the camera is kept as the master and never projected. The prints from the original, called 'rushes', can be either in black and white or in colour. Having the rushes printed in monochrome saves money, but can be a severe handicap at the editing stage, for sometimes colour changes in the subject matter are critical.

8mm enthusiasts have to use film stocks less suitable for making large numbers of prints, but Kodachrome II can be copied and the original kept as a master.

It is much less confusing for the laboratories, and films are less likely to go astray, if all exposed film is sent at regular intervals through one club or society member. Before dispatch he should make sure that each cameraman has numbered and labelled his rolls clearly, and to avoid duplication of numbers he may find it convenient to issue each cameraman with a batch of numbers: 1 to 20, 21 to 40, and so on. Any rolls for special processing, those that have to be force-developed one stop, for example, should be taped in a separate bundle with instructions attached. At the same time printing instructions should be clearly stated: that the rushes are to be in black and white or in colour, for instance. If facilities are already available for cutting the master, the instructions can request that the original be returned with the rushes. Otherwise it is better to try to find sufficient funds to cover the cost of having the master cut at the laboratories, and in this case the laboratories can be instructed to retain the original film until such time as shooting is complete.

GETTING EFFECTS AND MUSIC ON TRACK

With 16mm film shot at 24fps it is usually worth paying for outside professional help, unless the society's members also include a number of electronic wizards with a lot of equipment at their disposal.

Some film laboratories have their own film-recording theatres and editing facilities, so it is a good idea to keep the entire production of a club film with one firm. However, the hire of the studio is an expensive business and careful preparations have to be made beforehand to avoid wasting time. Every sound required for the track must be available on tape or disc (some already on magnetic film, as we shall see), and commentary should be checked to see that it fits picture.

Effects fall into the two categories described earlier: general bands of atmosphere, and specific effects that have to be in synchronization with the picture. The atmosphere tracks can be kept on tape at 7½ips and played in during the mixing of the sound track (see page 201). Each tape should run for a little more than the length of the section for which it is required, and they should be joined up in the correct order with bands of coloured spacing between each track. When there are a lot of atmosphere tracks, one following immediately on another, they should be made up into two reels, as described in Chapter 13, page 183. Very short bands of atmosphere covering one shot of, say, six or seven seconds should be treated as a laid effect (see below).

Effects that have to be synchronized with the picture must first be transferred to 16mm sprocketed magnetic film, and then laid on a special machine to match the picture. This means hiring a cutting-room and a professional editor, a costly business, so it is as well to keep these effects to a minimum.

The effects for laying are prepared as follows. First, a complete tape is made up with the effects in the order in which they appear in the film. Each one is identified at the front by recording a brief announcement; and there must always be more than enough of the required effect, to allow for mistakes in the cutting-room. If, for instance, the film shows a man hitting a post into the ground with five blows, the editor likes to have it recorded seven or eight times. The recordings should be made at a good level: it is better for them to be too high (but not so high as to be distorted) than too low, even though the subject may look distant in the picture. A high level can always be adjusted when the tracks are mixed, but any attempt to increase the level of a poor original recording only heightens unwanted electronic noise and tape hiss.

By this time there should be a detailed shot list in existence, describing each film shot and giving the cumulative running footage at each cut. This footage should be in the equivalent 35mm feet; all dubbing theatres work to that unit as it is more precise than 16mm footages. If there is no 16mm or 35mm footage counter available, the film can be measured on a bench with a ruler and the figures converted to 35mm equivalents by multiplying by 2½, but this is a very laborious method.

A copy of the shot list is given to the sound editor who is laying the special effects, and notes are made against any shot having associated laid effects. The sound editor needs to have the work print or cutting copy of the film in order to synchronize each effect, so it is important to make sure that all other preparations in connection with the film have been completed before the print is released to him.

A shot list therefore reads something like this:

	Vision	*Ft*	*Sound (notes)*
1	CS Axe biting into tree	0	Seven axe blows to be laid
2	MS Forester using axe	4	
3	MWA Base of oak: two foresters with axes	9	

Where music is restricted to beginning and end title sequences and the placing of this music does not have to be accurate to a single beat, then it is usually possible to play it in direct from disc at the time the final sound track is mixed. However, where a chord or a phrase in the middle of a music section has to match action precisely, then it has to be laid. Here exactly the same procedure is used as with the laying of effects, except that the music can be transferred directly from disc to magnetic film at the studio without going through the tape stage.

COMMENTARY AND FINAL MIXING

The commentary is sometimes recorded on the same day as, and immediately before, the final mixing of the sound track, and in fact this is rather convenient since the dubbing mixer has then had a chance to watch the film through a couple of times to get the feel of it.

A fellow member of the society with a good voice and delivery, or even a professional, may have been chosen to record the commentary, but in both cases the words should have been carefully timed beforehand and cue footages for the start of each paragraph written on the commentary script. These can be found by having an experimental read-through before going to the studio, and noting at which point it is necessary to start each paragraph so that key words come up at matching points in the action. The end footages should be worked out at the same time; these will be needed later, at the final stage of mixing the sound track.

At the commentator's preliminary read-through in the studio, it may be necessary to adjust some of the start footages if the rate of delivery is different from the rehearsal speed used beforehand. The actual end footages of each paragraph will then have to be adjusted, too. When 'rock and roll' machinery is being used, it is very easy to make last-minute timing alterations as the recording progresses, for the film can be wound backwards (with the recording track in synchronization) to the beginning of the paragraph in which the mistake has been made. This operation is carried out quite quickly.

When the commentary has been successfully recorded, all the elements necessary for the final sound track are available. The commentary is on one piece of track, the laid effects (already synchronized) on another one or two tracks, music is on another track or will come from disc, and atmosphere sound will come from one or two reels of tape. To help marry all these together, the dubbing mixer uses a dubbing chart (Fig 32), and most of the information on this is prepared beforehand in the film cutting-room. A full shot list on the dubbing chart is not necessary, but a brief summary of the action is a useful guide, with appropriate footages. The incoming and outgoing footages for all the laid-sound tracks are written in parallel vertical columns; the tape and disc cues are also given separate columns, and commentary footages are pencilled in. Some dubbing mixers arrange their charts on a horizontal basis, so it is important to find out in advance which system is used. Some firms supply blank charts on which the details can be filled in.

If there are a lot of tracks and tapes, the mixer may decide to premix some of them and add the remaining tracks on the second run-through. If he is dealing simply with a commentary, a laid-effects track and some tape, he is most likely to cope with everything in one operation, though he may wish to rehearse it before he is ready to try a recording.

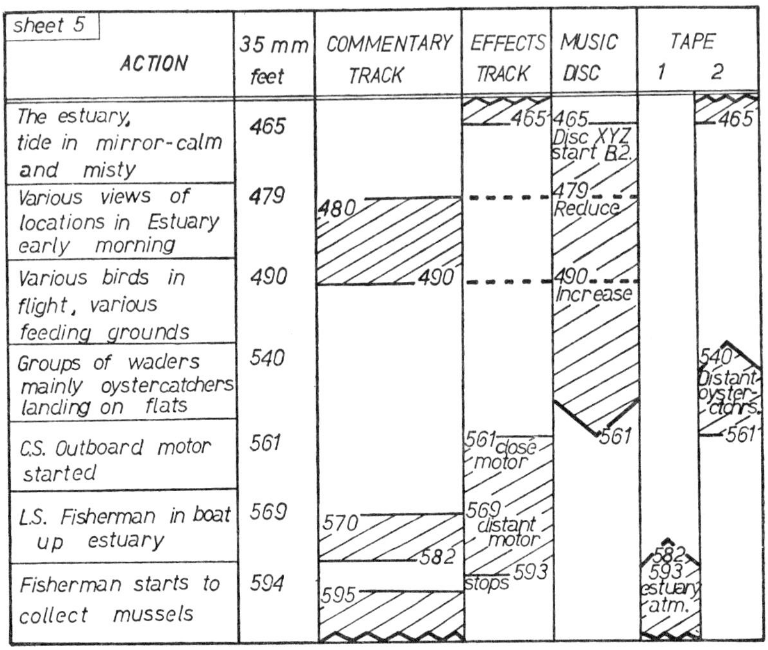

Fig 32 Dubbing chart for use in professional studio

The time taken for dubbing varies tremendously with the complexity of the film, but the commentary recording and final mix of a twenty-minute film could be done in one half-day session, assuming that all the preparations have been made thoroughly.

The final mixed track is made on 16mm magnetic film, and this master recording can be used for transfer either directly onto a stripe on the show print, or if optical tracks are required for projection the master is transferred first to an optical track negative. From this and the cut picture master the final show prints are made by the laboratories.

THE ACTION MASTER

The original Ektachrome or the Eastmancolor negative may be cut and matched to the work print either by the club production group or at the laboratories. If this is done at the laboratories, all opticals such as dissolves and fades must be

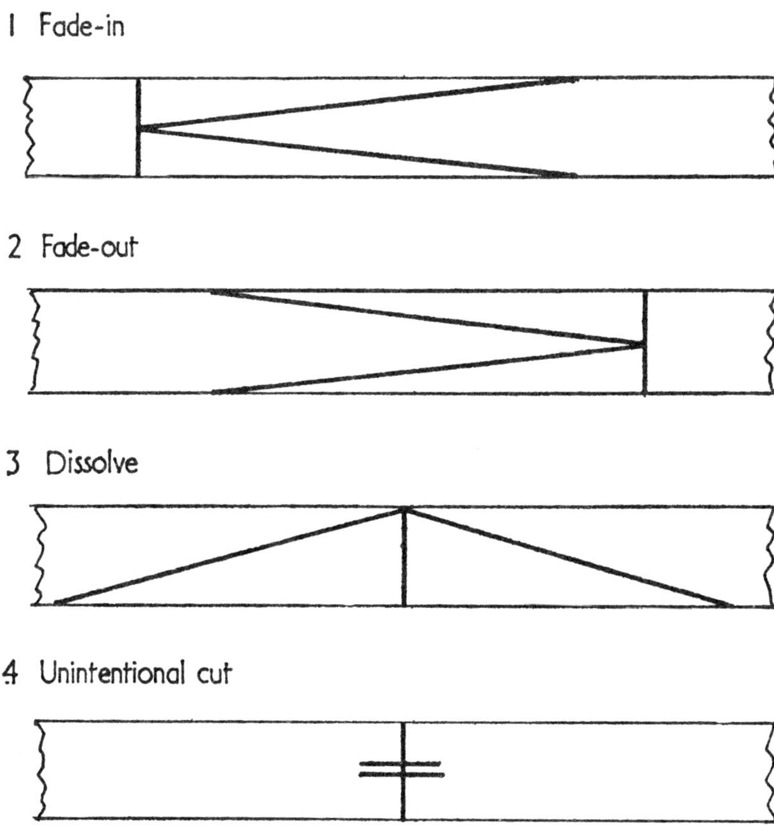

Fig 33 How to mark work prints for the laboratory

marked on the work print in chinagraph pencil, using the standard code (Fig 33). When the original is cut outside the laboratories, extreme care must be taken in handling it and keeping it dust free; the emulsions are soft and scratch easily, and the celluloid base often gets charged with static electricity, which attracts dust particles and makes a dirty print.

The simplest and cheapest way to cut the original is to make up one complete roll which matches the work print, frame for frame. The matching is done by comparing the edge numbers on the side of the original with the same numbers on the work print, which should have been printed through on to it. But joining the shots into one roll has two big disadvantages. Firstly, the film joins between consecutive shots are always on the picture area, and print through to some extent. Secondly, optical effects such as dissolves and title superimpositions have to be made first and cut into the original, instead of being made in the printing process. However, if cash is short and there are no opticals, this cheaper method may be preferred.

A much better way of providing for opticals is to cut the original into A and B rolls (Fig 34), in which sequences on either side of dissolves appear on alternate rolls. The two scenes that are to dissolve into one another are overlapped by the length of the dissolve, and between the end of one dissolve and the beginning of the next one roll always has blank spacing equivalent to the total length of action frames on the other roll. But even with this method film splices are visible in sequences between dissolves. They can be entirely avoided by the more expensive checkerboard system (Fig 35).

In this system, alternate shots are placed on A and B rolls, whether they are cuts or dissolves, and *black* spacing is used. Care must always be taken to make an overlap on the spacing side of every join so that this never shows even when the two rolls are printed one after the other onto the same piece of

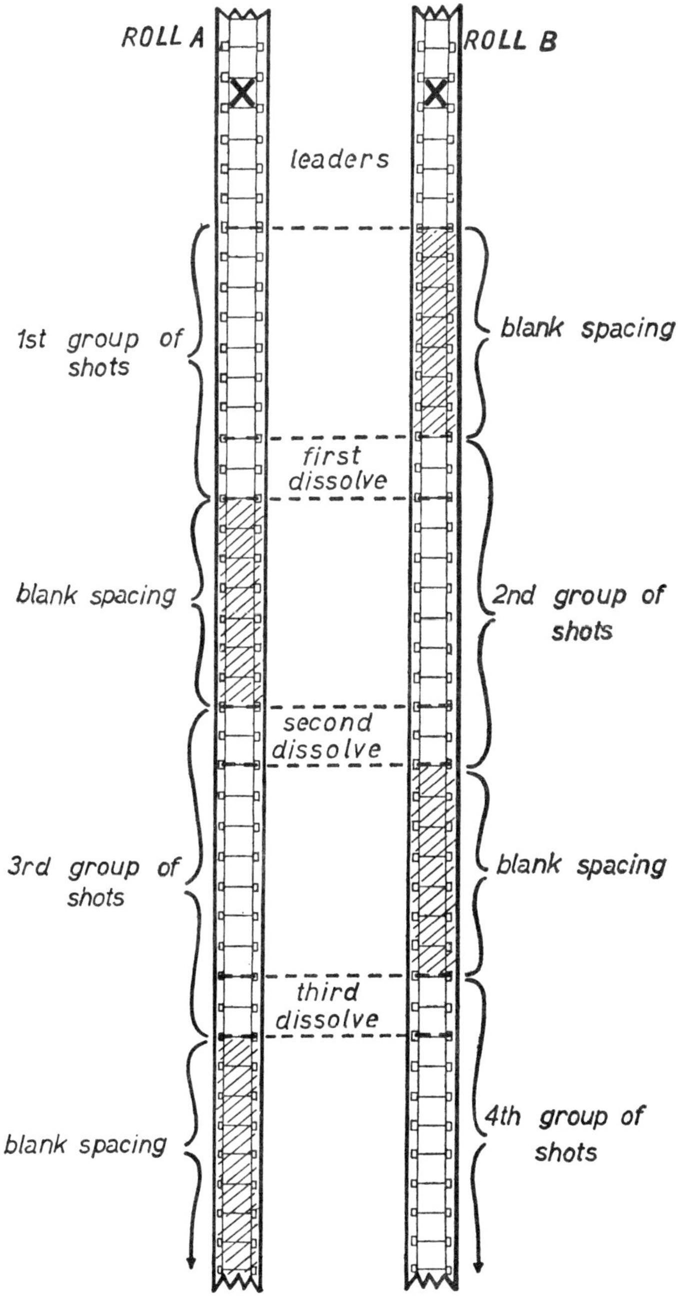

Fig 34 Making up original into A and B rolls for printing

print stock. Dissolves and other effects can be made in the same way by overlapping as for A and B roll printing.

It is only practicable to cut the original in this way if an editing bench and a four-way synchronizer are available. A synchronizer is a set of sprocketed wheels which enables several 16mm films to be wound through simultaneously and in perfect co-ordination, and has a frame and footage counter incorporated into it. If this piece of equipment is not available, it is better to pay for the laboratories to cut the original. Although the matching *can* be done without a synchronizer, it is an extremely laborious business and there is a high risk of the original being scratched.

TITLES

Title sequences are usually such that the lettering appears superimposed on the action, either over the first two or three shots or over a group of shots a short distance in from the beginning and following a 'teaser'. Teasers are commonly used in television films, where the producer is anxious to capture the attention of the viewer at an early stage and persuade him to watch the rest of the programme.

When a film is made for a captive audience, there is much to be said for a set of titles, nicely designed in their own right, which can be photographed separately and cut on before the main action begins. If the film is to be shown at natural history society meetings, there is bound to be a difficult fifteen seconds or so while the lights are being switched off, the audience stops talking, and the projectionist finds focus (he should have checked this before the audience arrived, but invariably has not). A main title sequence without important action is therefore not a bad thing.

If it is decided to superimpose titles over action, the lettering should be painted on matt black card, and when these are photographed the exposure must be such that the background

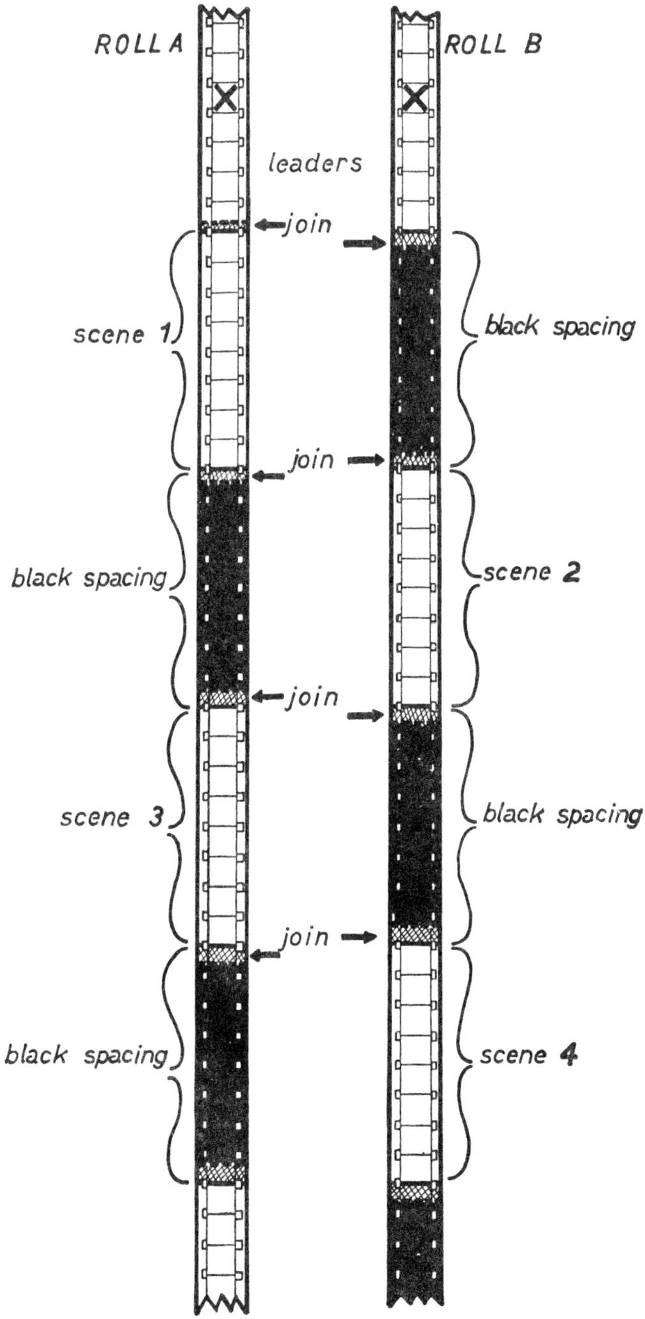

Fig 35 Making up original for checkerboard printing

really is jet black. If a good artist cannot be afforded, Lettraset is very useful. Even though the film may be in colour, it is often the case that white or pale yellow letters are best for superimposition work, unless there happens to be a lot of white in the background shot. If a bright colour is particularly desired, it is best to consult the laboratories first and to take their advice on whether or not the desired effect is likely to come off.

On reversal film, titles can be made up into A and B rolls in much the same way as for other optical effects, but with a negative/positive process the superimposition must be prepared first by the laboratories, and a new negative with the desired effect already photographed inserted into the cut negative.

THE SHOW PRINT

After the sound track has been mixed and the original film cut, a technician at the laboratories examines the cut original and grades it. He compares the densities of shots, and notes if there are any discrepancies between the colour of individual shots in the same sequence. He then programmes the printing machine for various lights and filters, so that the final print will be of constant density and the colours of grass, sky and flesh tones on consecutive shots will not vary.

To help the grader produce the right sort of print he is usually given a copy of the shot list, with details of the time of day at which certain sequences were shot and of any special effects. For example, one sequence might have been filmed late in the evening and a gradual transition to sunset is required. Unless informed of this, the grader may well try to remove the redness from the later shots and completely lose the evening effect.

The grader may be very skilled, but it is unlikely that the resultant first print will be exactly right: it is sometimes good enough for private purposes, but is not necessarily expected to be ready for public showing. So, on projection, this 'answer' print must be carefully scrutinized by the director and his team, and notes made of those shots that are not satisfactory. It is quite likely that the grader will have already noticed which shots need further attention, but in addition to the obvious points there may be some – subtle plumage colours, for example – that only the naturalists will be able to judge. All further comments and precise instructions for regrading are written on a copy of the shot list and returned to the grader with the answer print.

The team then sit back and wait for a week or so, hoping for the return of a perfect print – or perhaps already, fired with enthusiasm by the result of their first efforts, they are busy planning their next wildlife movie.

Glossary

ACKLE A word in use among natural history cine photographers, meaning to arrange subjects, scenery and so on, in front of the camera in a controlled set-up. Hence ackler, ackling.

ANSWER PRINT The first print of a new film for projection. Although it may sometimes be perfectly satisfactory for showing to an audience, the answer print usually reveals some imperfections in grading and colour balance which the producer may think worth rectifying before an important showing.

APERTURE The size of the lens iris, which determines the exposure of the film. In many modern cameras this is taken care of automatically.

ASSEMBLE To piece together all the shots of a film in a provisional order.

BIG CLOSE-UP An extreme close shot of a subject; in the case of mammal or human, showing only part of the head or some small detail of its anatomy.

BLIMP A special box that absorbs the mechanical sound of the camera, thus preventing it from disturbing animals being filmed. Particularly important for mammals.

BLIND American word for HIDE.

CAMERA ANGLE The angle at which the camera sees the subject.

CLOSE-UP Usually a shot showing just the face of a human

or animal, but could be some other detail: eg the hump on a camel's back.

COLOUR TEMPERATURE A measure of the quality of light from a particular source, whether it be artificial or the sun. Film stocks are manufactured for use with light of specific colour temperatures. Measured in degrees Kelvin.

COMMENTARY The spoken words, other than those that are part of the action, which make up part of the sound track of a documentary film.

CONTINUITY The consistency of dress, plumage, scenery, posture and so on, on either side of a cut between two shots.

COPY A reversal print made from a reversal original.

CUT The point at which one film shot is spliced to the next. To cut, *see* EDIT.

CUTAWAY A shot of somebody or something not in the main action story: eg a close-up of a birdwatcher using binoculars. A cutaway may be used to avoid a jump cut in the action.

CUTTING COPY A positive film used only for the purposes of editing.

DEPTH OF FIELD On any given aperture this is the difference between the minimum and maximum distances between which the subject is in focus.

DISSOLVE The merging of the end of one shot into the beginning of the next. Usually made at the laboratories during the printing stage, by fading out the first shot as the second shot is faded in.

DUBBING The process of re-recording sound; making a final film sound track from various other sources such as laid tracks, tape, disc and so on.

DUBBING THEATRE Film recording studio at which film sound tracks are made.

EDIT To join film shots together in the correct story order, and to cut them to their final length.

EFFECTS Recorded noises other than music and speech, for a film sound track.

EMULSION The light-sensitive coating on a film which bears the image after exposure and processing.

ESTABLISHING SHOT A shot used to establish a new scene, often a wide-angle shot in which all the characters in the action that follows are seen within the same frame.

EXPOSURE The amount of light allowed to reach each frame of film; controlled by the aperture setting.

EXTENSION TUBE A metal cylinder, one end of which may be screwed into the camera, the other end taking screwed-in lenses. Extension tubes increase the effective focal length of the lens, but as a result the lens/subject distance is drastically reduced. Therefore used for filming close-ups of very small things usually at ranges of a few inches (macro-photography).

FADE IN The gradual appearance, from total blackness, of a film shot.

FADE OUT The gradual disappearance into total blackness of a film shot.

FILTER Piece of coloured gelatine or glass, which may be mounted on the front of the lens, or between the lens and the film; used either to change the tones of a scene or to change the effective colour temperature of the light reaching the emulsion. May also be fitted on artificial lights to change their colour temperature.

FOCAL LENGTH The distance from the optical centre of a lens to the film, when the lens is focused at infinity.

FRAME A single picture on a length of cine film.

FRAME LINE The line that separates adjacent frames on a piece of cine film.

GATE The part of a camera or projector that holds a single frame of cine film during exposure or projection.

GRADING Estimating the amount and quality of light that must be used on each shot when the cut master is printed, so as to make an even print. The work is done by a grader at the film laboratories, who programmes the printing machine to carry out the necessary adjustments.

HIDE Small portable construction like a box-shaped tent, in which the cameraman works when filming many kinds of animal. *See* BLIND.

JOIN A splice between two shots.

JUMP CUT A cut between almost identical shots taken with the same lens and from the same camera angle. But because the subject is never in exactly the same position there is a resultant jump in action.

LAYING OF SOUND The process of arranging parts of a sound track in synchronization with the picture. Carried out by means of various magnetic film tracks before they are mixed together in a dubbing theatre.

LEADER The film that is laced into a camera projector or printer before the film proper begins.

LONG SHOT A distant shot showing the whole of the subject.

MACRO-PHOTOGRAPHY Close-up photography of tiny things by the use of extension tubes.

MARRIED PRINT A print that carries both the picture and the sound track in synchronization.

MASTER The original film as exposed in the camera.

MEDIUM SHOT A shot that shows the major part of a subject; in human terms, head and shoulders and down to about waistline.

MIX *See* DISSOLVE. In sound work: to combine several tracks together to make a film sound track.

MONTAGE Creative editing. Also used to denote a series of fast cut or dissolved shots suggesting a journey or the passage of time or events.

MOOD MUSIC Specially recorded music for plays, films and television, classified under various mood headings.

MUTE A film that does not as yet have a sound track.

NARRATION Strictly, commentary by someone involved in the film action; now often synonymous with commentary.

NEGATIVE Original film exposed in the camera, from which positive prints may be made.

OPTICALS Special effects made during the printing of a film, such as fades, dissolves and superimpositions.

PAN A shot in which the camera moves about its vertical axis; to move the camera in such a way whilst filming.

POST-SYNCHRONIZATION Recording sound to a shot or a complete film after it has been filmed.

REFLEX VIEWFINDER Viewfinder in which the subject is viewed via the taking lens of the camera.

REVERSAL FILM Film stock that produces a positive image after processing.

ROUGH CUT The first rough assembly of the shots of a film, all joined in their approximate order but without any fine cutting having been made on them.

RUSHES Film straight from the laboratory after processing. Usually applied to the prints from the camera original which will subsequently be used for editing.

SCENE Where the action happens. In any one scene the director may choose to photograph the action in a number of different shots.

SEQUENCE A group of scenes forming a recognizable film 'paragraph'.

SHOT One continuous run of the cine camera to photograph a piece of action or a static view.

SLOW MOTION The slowing down of the action by running the camera faster than normal during filming.

SOUND TRACK The path on the side of a cine film that carries the sound information. Can either be an optical track made of the same photographic materials as the picture, or a magnetic track on a stripe of iron oxide.

SPACING Blank cine film used in the cutting-room for leaders, and for spacing out laid sounds on tracks.

SPIDER Device for holding tripod legs steady on an otherwise smooth and slippery surface.

STRIPE A thin band of iron oxide down the side of a film, enabling a magnetic sound track to be recorded.

SYNCHRONIZER Apparatus through which two or more films can be wound in step with one another. Used for cutting original film to match a cutting copy, and for laying sound tracks.

TAKE A single shot. If the first attempt at a shot is unsuccessful and the action, camera position, lens and so on, are the same, the second attempt will be the same shot but the second take.

TILT To rotate the camera about its horizontal axis.

TRACK To move the camera *bodily* during the taking of a shot; in sound, a roll of film bearing one of the elements of the final sound track (ie commentary, music, effects) before it is mixed.

WILD TRACK Any film sound recorded non-synchronously.

WORK PRINT *See* CUTTING COPY.

ZOOM To operate a zoom lens during filming so that the subject appears to be moving closer or farther away from camera.

ZOOM LENS A lens of variable focal length.

Further Reading

Baddeley, W. Hugh. *The Technique of Documentary Film Production*. Focal Press, 1970.
Branston, Brian. *A Film Maker's Guide*. George Allen & Unwin Ltd, 1967.
Couffer, Jack. *Song of Wild Laughter*. Constable & Co, 1963.
Eastman, Rosemary. *The Kingfisher*. Collins, 1969.
Gooders, John. *Where to Watch Birds*. Sphere Books Ltd, reprint May 1971.
Jackman, Leslie. *Marine Aquaria*. David & Charles, 1968.
Reade, Winwood, and Stuttard, R. M., editors. *A Handbook for Naturalists*. Council for Nature and Evans Bros Ltd, 1968.
Soper, Tony. *The Bird Table Book*. David & Charles, 1965.
Tweedie, Michael. *Pleasure from Insects*. David & Charles, 1968.
Warham, John. *The Technique of Wildlife Cinematography*. Focal Press, 1966.
Also various Focal Cinebooks: *How to Edit*, *How to Script*, etc.

The *Encyclopaedia of Tape Recording*, Number 1, August 1970, contains useful information for the wildlife cameraman. This issue is entitled *Natural History Sound Recording* (author Richard Margoschis) and can be obtained from the publishers, Print & Press Services Limited, 17 Alverstone Avenue, East Barnet, Hertfordshire.

Acknowledgements

I AM not going to try to list all those who have made contributions to this book: the list is too long. Many wildlife cameramen and television colleagues have discussed problems and techniques with me over the years, and inevitably much of their experience has found its way into this book; indeed, that was one of the purposes of writing it.

I hope that all the unnamed contributors will forgive me if I restrict my acknowledgements to those who have given special help with the preparation of the manuscript. They are Gerald Thompson and Peter Parks of Oxford Scientific Films, Eric Ashby, Leslie Jackman, Ronald Peggs and Ronald Eastman. Jeffery Boswall and Hugh Falkus kindly allowed me to quote extracts from their scripts.

My thanks are also due to George Shears, film cameraman at the Bristol Production Centre of the British Broadcasting Corporation, for checking technical data, to my assistant Sheila Fullom for making many valuable suggestions on the improvement of the text, and to Elizabeth Todd and Caroline Ford for making the line drawings.

Index

Numbers in bold refer to plates